FULL COLOR

Planner for A Magical 2026

Amy Cesari

Be a fire-safe witch!

Lots of space above and around the flame.

Candle is on a fire-safe dish.

Never leave flames unattended.

Be a pet-safe witch!

Some essential oils and herbs (like cinnamon) and even salt and candles can be dangerous for our pets. Research, be cautious, and don't leave spell ingredients unattended.

COPYRIGHT & GENERAL DISCLAIMER:
PLANNER FOR A MAGICAL 2026 - FULL COLOR
ALL TEXT AND IMAGES © 2025 BOOK OF SHADOWS LLC, AMY CESARI

THIS BOOK DOES NOT CONTAIN MEDICAL ADVICE AND DOES NOT INTEND TO TREAT OR DIAGNOSE MEDICAL OR HEALTH ISSUES. ALWAYS SEEK PROFESSIONAL MEDICAL TREATMENT. AND DON'T EAT OR USE PLANTS IF YOU DON'T KNOW WHAT THEY ARE.

ALL RIGHTS RESERVED: For personal use only. No parts of this book may be reproduced, copied, or transmitted in any form, by any means, including photocopying, recording, or other electronic or mechanical methods, without the prior written permission of the author, except in the case of brief quotations for critical reviews and certain other noncommercial uses permitted by copyright law.
ETHICS: Where do your magical supplies come from? Please research the origins and ethical use of any plants, crystals, or animal remains (bones, skulls, horns, and feathers) that you use in your magic.
DISCLAIMER OF LIABILITY: This book is for informational and entertainment purposes only and is not intended as a substitute for medical, financial, spiritual, or life advice of any kind. Like any craft involving flames, the power of your mind unhinged, eating plants and herbs, and the unyielding forces of the universe, Witchcraft poses some inherent risk. The author and publisher are not liable or responsible for any outcome of magical spells performed from this book or otherwise. Readers agree to cast spells, work with fire, ingest herbs, soak in bath salts, light candles and incense, channel deities, use spirit boards, and perform any and all other magical practices at their own risk. The images in this book are for decorative purposes—they are not realistic guides for arranging flame-based altars. Be fire-safe and never leave flaming things or incense unattended. Readers of this book take full responsibility when using fire. Readers accept full personal risk and responsibility for the outcome, consequence, and magic of any spells they cast. This book is not for children. And so it shall be.

Write three intentions or three words of focus on these three books.

This Magical Year Belongs To:

Hail and Welcome to Your Magical 2026

Magic?! It's Your Life!

Magic is a way to influence your destiny, using the powers within you and around you, like the moon, the stars, the sun, and the elements of Earth, Air, Fire, Water, & Aether.

A witch's home can also hold its own magical power, as if it has a life of its own. You can create and nurture your home's spirit or energy with simple rituals, charms, and spells. In turn, your house becomes a sacred space that helps you cultivate your magic.

It's not the size of your house that makes it magical. It's you. You might have just one room, one windowsill, a suitcase, or a hidden altar to work your magic. That's enough.

The magic of "home" is a space to be yourself just as you are. Yet it's also a place to discover yourself on a deeper level. Home can spark the magic to create, to dream about planting a garden, or to clear space for a new hobby. And if you don't yet have that place where you feel safe to be your magical self, you'll get there. You absolutely deserve it!

As a witch, you may find yourself naturally drawn to simple magic and daily rituals like lighting incense and candles to renew your spirit, filling your kitchen with magical meals, or gazing at the moon and stars—wishing that tomorrow holds a brighter day.

All of this is magic! And a secret to being a powerful witch is knowing yourself in the present moment, remembering that you have the power to influence your destiny.

To do this, be honest about your desires, your fears, your darkness, and your light. Do this consistently, and you will make magic happen. You already hold this power within you. It's yours! You're ready! So... let's try it...

Making Every Day Magical

1. Pretend you are the beloved and witchy main character of a magical book (or movie). See yourself and your situation exactly as you are today from an outsider's point of view (as if someone is reading about you in a book—this is your "reader!").

2. Your reader is rooting for your success! How do they see you and what do they love about you? Are you quirky? Snarky? Quiet yet powerful? A sage crone? Who are you at your most beloved and authentic self right now? This is your place of power. Feel that within.

3. From this inner power, what will you do next?! How will you overcome any obstacles? What'll make magic unfold for you (and your reader) in the next chapter?

4. When you find the glimmer or spark that lights you up and makes you want to take one step of action (even if it's simple or obvious), this is a clue. Take that one step. This is your intuition, your true self, the part of you that knows what you desire and how to succeed.

5. Repeat this spell daily or anytime you need to re-spark the magic in your life.

So... are you ready? Hope so! Magic can and will unfold for you this year, so believe it, and keep moving forward... one magical step at a time.

Tips to Use This Planner

1. Familiarize yourself with the introduction and basics of magic and spellcasting.
2. Fill out the "MAGICAL VISION" planning pages at the end of the introduction.
3. Try to perform the "big spell" or one of the mini-spells in this book each month.
4. Review your MAGICAL VISION monthly, whenever you like, or on the new moons. Adjust as needed. Break your goals into smaller intentions and actions for each month, and take small, purposeful actions forward if desired, step by step.
5. Repeat this process for as many of the 12 months of the year as you can to "stir the cauldron" and see what happens... (...Will magic happen?! Let's hope so!)

Goals, Plans, and Intentions

Yes, this is a planner, but that doesn't mean you have to get intense about... planning. You can even plan to do less this year. In fact, that's a great idea. Get to know what *you* want (not your family, not society, etc...) and then use the powers of magic and intention to focus your energy on those things. Here are some tips:

- Less is more. Go for broader feelings and intentions rather than super specific dates, processes, and outcomes. Leave room for magic to surprise you in fantastic ways.
- Make your goals as big or small as you want.
- Instead of saying what you don't want, "to stop being an emotional wreck," phrase it positively so you feel good when you say it, "to feel at ease with all of my emotions."
- Think of plans you make as guidelines. Don't be afraid to scrap them and do something else if they don't feel right anymore. It's never too late to change directions or make new plans—in fact, that's often where the real magic comes into play.

About This Book

- Write & doodle in this book! Expressing your thoughts in writing is a powerful way to create your reality. Here are some ideas: *Your day-to-day-mundane appointments. Daily gratitude. Daily reflections. Daily tarot. A diary of your spiritual journey. Intuitive messages. How you feel during different moon phases.*
- "Spellcasting Basics" are included if you're brand new to magic. Please read this if so.
- And remember, the magic is inside you. Even if you start this book "late" or if it's not "the best" moon phase for a spell, you are the real power in your magical life.

How do you make your house magical?! By doing simple, small things that tuck magic and intention into the corners of your home.

Every part of your home, whether or not it looks "witchy," carries an energy, a vibe, and a potential for enchantment. Each room, corner, shelf, and doorway is alive with symbolism and magical opportunity—no matter how simple.

House magic isn't just about aesthetics or function. It's about shaping energy and creating a unique sanctuary that supports your spirit and personal power.

When you bless, clean, decorate, or rearrange your space, you are practicing house magic. Your broom becomes a wand, your pantry a potion shelf, and your bed an altar of dreams. Every space in your home can be sacred space.

And your magic doesn't have to be out in the open — plenty of witches conceal their magic and keep it private, even in their homes.

You might place crystals near doorways, light candles to shift the mood, or set magical intentions when you sweep.

Create rituals when making your bed, cooking a meal, or opening a window to let in fresh air. Maybe you keep a deck of tarot cards, a notebook, and a pen at your altar for daily divinations or place flowers on your table to set a bright mood.

What matters most is how your home makes you feel. Is your space comforting, creative, and magical? If not, how can you shift the energy?

Is there a scent, color, sound, or intention that will align your home with the life you desire?

Set an intention to work with the magic of your house this year. Be present, and make small, purposeful changes so your home reflects who you are and what you might desire in the future.

Do this, and you'll find that your home quickly becomes more than a shelter... it becomes a living, breathing spell of your own making.

BLESSING
- AND CLEANSING -
THE ENERGY OF YOUR HOME

House blessing spells are so versatile and effective, you might find it's the kind of spell you use the most. Your home can absorb energy, both heavy and light. A house blessing or cleansing will help you clear, refresh, and re-set the energy of your home in accordance with the intention and "vibe" that you desire.

A "classic" house blessing or elemental cleansing spell involves the four (or five!) elements, a candle or other representation of fire; incense smoke, bells or clapping for air; water; and salt for earth. However, you can use just one of these elements or mix and match depending on what you have on hand or what works for you.

To begin, it's best to open some doors and windows to let energy flow. Place all of your elemental correspondences on your altar or in a central spot (read ahead to the "February" spellwork for more on altars).

Light a candle, if possible. With your salt or another representation of "earth," walk through your space, sprinkling a little salt in all the corners, doorways and windowsills while chanting the incantation on the facing page (or words of your choosing).

Repeat and continue walking through the house for the other four elements, burning incense, wafting a feather, or ringing a bell for the element of air, carrying the lit candle (or representation of the sun like bright yellow flowers) for fire, sprinkling water or moon water for water, and just passing through as your magical self, if you choose to use the fifth element of spirit or aether.

When you are finished with each pass, say a final intention, something like,

By the power of the elements, the sun, moon, and stars, may the energy be clear and clean.
I consecrate this space as my own.
And so it shall be.

Let the candles and incense burn out on their own or snuff them out purposefully. Repeat this spell or a variation of it whenever you need to freshen up your home, after you've had guests or an argument, or anytime the energy of your house begins to feel stagnant or uneasy.

OTHER WAYS TO BLESS YOUR HOME:

LEMON-ROSEMARY SIMMER POT: Simmer water with lemon slices, rosemary, and cloves to cleanse stagnant energy through the power of magical scents.

HERBAL FLOOR WASH: Mop with moon-charged water mixed with a pinch of salt and a few drops of pet-safe essential oil (or a sprig of lavender or basil tossed in).

SIGILS & SYMBOLS: Circle your house counterclockwise three times, then clockwise three times as you use chalk, oil, or lemon juice to draw protective sigils above thresholds, on door frames, and on windows.

DAILY SWEEPING RITUAL: Sweep out the door each day with the intention of clearing old energy and welcoming in the new.

And of course, create your own blessing ritual by adapting these ideas or coming up with something new. The most powerful magic comes from your authentic presence aligned with true intentions from your soul.

Smoke of air & fire of earth
Blessed be this home & hearth
Drive away all harm and fear
Only good may enter here.

— Author Unknown

HOUSEHOLD OBJECTS

Not a complete list. Add your own!

MORTAR & PESTLE — Abundance, fertility, alchemy, & creative potential.

Water JUGS symbolize life and our connection to the elements.

SCISSORS signify release & change.

NEEDLE & thread — A symbol of mending and healing.

Mirrors — The moon, the spirit world, & reflections of the divinity within.

CANDLES & MATCHES are symbols of spirit, light, prayer, and the element of fire.

KEYS unlock potential.

House Plants — Remind us of our connection to nature.

HOUSE MAGIC

Altar
A spiritual center for your home or practice.

Besom
Hang a broom as a classic energetic protection spell.

Door Wreaths
Hang circular wreaths & interlocking symbols for energetic protection.

Art
Use witchy art & signage to set a magical mood.

Blue or Purple Door
A sign that "a witch lives here" & a bit of "color magic."

Statues
Representations of deities & animals evoke their energies.

Symbols
Moons, pentacles, & cauldrons... choose your favorites!

Are you out of the "broom closet?" Is your witchcraft on full display in your home? There's lots you can do to visibly enchant your space and make your witchcraft an integrated part of your home's functionality and decor.

& HIDDEN SPELLS

Moon Spells
Look up at night to remember that magic is always there.

Secret Sigils
Hide symbols in concealed places like under furniture, rugs, or on top of doors.

HERBS
Nothing to see here! Just a well-stocked spice cabinet and a thriving herb garden.

BOUQUETS
hold hidden magic and energetics with the symbolism of plants & flowers.

MATCHBOX Altars
Keep your altar in a cute little box that you can take out when it's time for rituals.

CRYSTALS
Bury crystals, hide them in your attic or cellar, or hang them as sun catchers.

Potpourri
Tuck herbal charms in drawers & closets... powerful & discreet.

Do you keep your witchcraft under wraps? All good! It can feel powerful, sacred, and special to keep your magic hidden. Here are some ideas, but of course, the opportunities for secret magic are endless and up to you.

The days of the week correspond to ancient planetary symbolism and energy. While you might enjoy aligning yourself with the planetary power of specific days of the week for specific spells or intentions, this correspondence is entirely optional. Cast your magic on any day that feels appropriate and powerful to you and to your schedule.

HOURS OF THE DAY

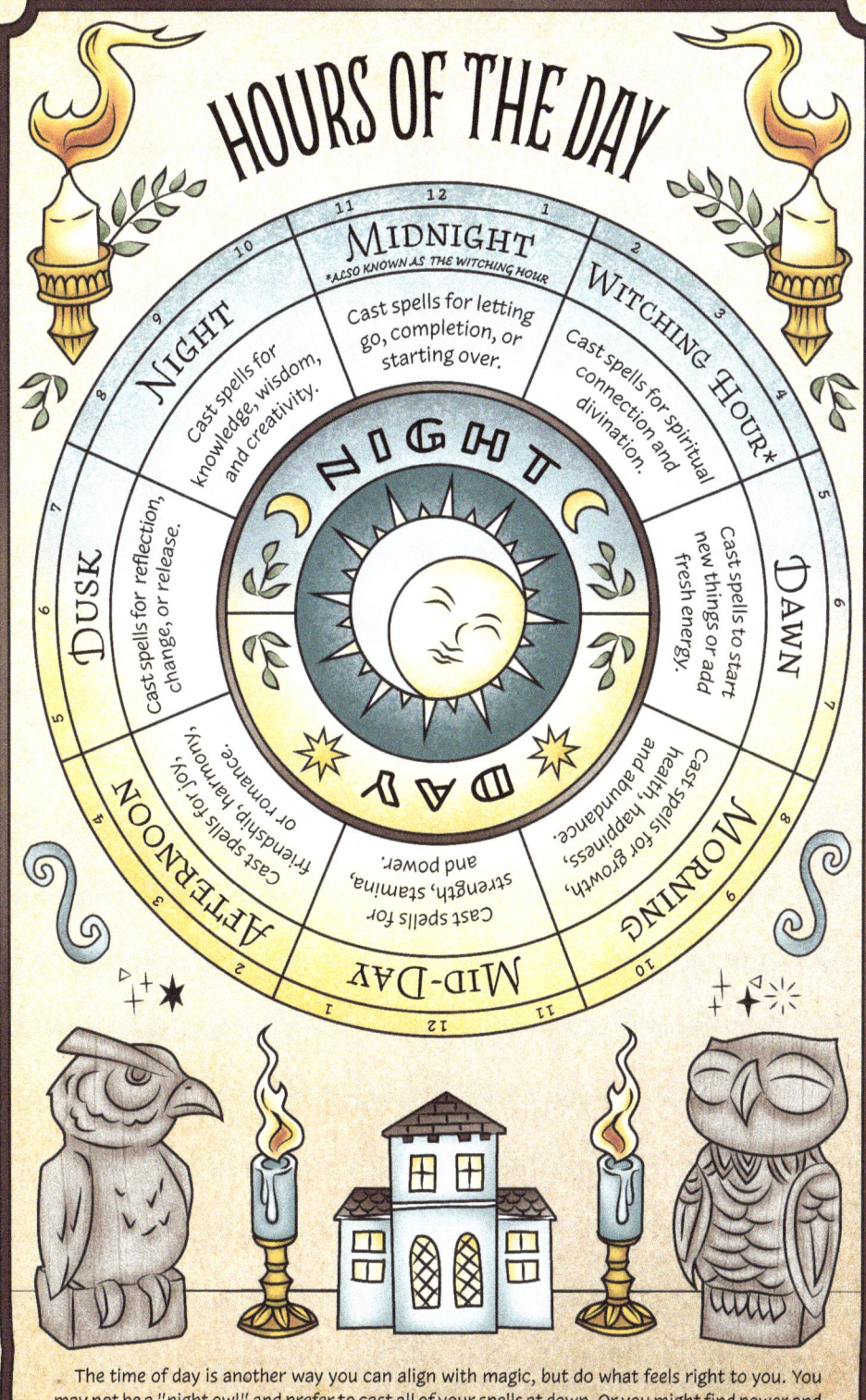

The time of day is another way you can align with magic, but do what feels right to you. You may not be a "night owl" and prefer to cast all of your spells at dawn. Or you might find power and pleasure in precisely lining up the moon phase, the season, the day of the week, and time of the day to cast your spells. Either method is correct, it all depends on you and how you prefer to work.

MAGICAL HERBS

Not a complete list. Add your own!

CLEARING
Use these herbs to help you shift the vibe.

BENZOIN · **CEDAR** · **HYSSOP** · **MINT** · **PINE** · **VERBENA**

LOVE & PEACE
Looking for love? These herbs can help you cultivate the mood.

BASIL · **CINNAMON** · **CLOVES** · **LAVENDER** · **ROSE** · **VERBENA**

PROTECTION
Keep your home's energy secured with these time-tested protective herbs.

AGRIMONY · **FENNEL** · **HEATHER** · **MULLEIN** · **ROSEMARY** · **RUE** (POISON)

& CRYSTALS

CLEARING

Place these crystals in your home to clear stagnant energy.

Not a complete list. Add your own!

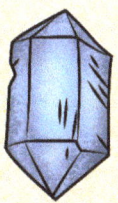

AMAZONITE **BERYL** **FUCHSITE** **KYANITE** **JET**

ANTI-ANXIETY

Use these crystals to keep calm... and carry on.

AMETHYST **CALCITE** **FLUORITE** **HOWLITE** **RUBY**

PROTECTION

Place these crystals near doors or in corners to make your home an energetic fortress.

HAGSTONE **OBSIDIAN** **ONYX** **SMOKY QUARTZ** **SALT**

the correspondence of
THE MOON AND SEASONS

The moon completes a full cycle of its phases in just over 28 days, which is relatively quick. One moon cycle is perfect for shorter projects and immediate goals.

You can also correspond these shorter moon phases to a longer-term cycle, the seasons, also known as the Wheel of the Year. This longer cycle is useful for "big" goals and plans that'll take more than a month.

While the seasons and sun embody more of a conscious or outward energy, the moon is subconscious or internal. However, they both follow a similar cycle and progression of dark to light.

The handy chart on the following page demonstrates that the phases of the moon correspond to an energy point on the Wheel of the Year. This pattern of energy—the waxing and waning of light—is no coincidence. It's the pattern and flow of the creative force of the universe. This process and cycle is how magic "works."

Here's an overview of the eight sabbats and a chart that connects them to the moon phases and seasons.

IMBOLC: February 1 or 2. Imbolc is the time to celebrate the first signs of spring or the return of the sun's increasing light. This sabbat corresponds to the waxing crescent moon.

OSTARA: March 20. This sabbat is celebrated on the spring equinox. Witches often mark this day with a ritual planting of seeds. Ostara corresponds to the first quarter moon.

BELTANE: May 1. Beltane is a time for rituals of growth, creation, and taking action to make things happen. This sabbat corresponds to the waxing gibbous moon.

LITHA: June 20. This sabbat celebrates the summer solstice, when the sun is at its strongest. Litha is a time of great magical and personal power and corresponds to the full moon.

LUGHNASADH: August 1. This day is a celebration of the "first harvest" where we gather early grains, herbs, fruits, and vegetables from the earth. It corresponds to the waning gibbous moon, where light and power begin to descend from their fullest stage.

MABON: September 21. Celebrated on the autumnal equinox, this sabbat is about release, balance, and letting go. It is the second harvest and corresponds to the last quarter moon.

SAMHAIN: October 31. Samhain is a celebration of the dark half of the year. It is a time to cast spells of protection for the upcoming winter. It corresponds to the waning crescent moon.

YULE: December 21. Marked by the winter solstice and the shortest (darkest) day of the year, this sabbat corresponds to the dark and new moon.

A NOTE ABOUT THE CROSS-QUARTER DATES AND SOUTHERN HEMISPHERE SEASONS:

CROSS QUARTER DATES: The dates for the two solstices and two equinoxes each year—Ostara, Litha, Mabon, and Yule—are calculated astronomically from the position of the earth to the sun. The "cross quarter" festivals, which are the points between—Imbolc, Beltane, Lughnasadh, and Samhain—are often celebrated on "fixed" dates instead of the actual midpoints. This book lists both the "Fixed Festival Dates," when it's more common to celebrate, and the "Astronomical Dates." Choose either date or any time in between for your own ritual. 'Tis the season for magic.

SOUTHERN HEMISPHERE SEASONS: If you're on the "southern" half of the Earth, like in Australia, the seasonal shifts are opposite on the calendar year. So you'll feel the energy of the summer solstice (corresponding to the full moon) in December instead of June, and so on.

THE SECRETS OF

YOUR FEELINGS ARE THE SECRET SAUCE

An intention is when you strongly feel what you desire in your body, as if you already have it. To make real magic happen, combine actions (things that you do), intentions (also known as feelings or emotions), as well as powers outside of yourself, such as the moon and nature. This chart will give you some ideas on how to feel and set your intentions.

You can use the phases of the moon to "pull the thread" of magic forward by listening to your feelings and continually refocusing these intentions with actions to match.

Since the moon and emotions are both linked to the subconscious, you'll use your body to feel these things and set intentions, not your thoughts in your conscious mind.

First Quarter
Feel where you would like to change, grow, or expand. Allow yourself to dream and imagine what it might be like to make a change, even if it doesn't seem possible right now.

Waxing Moon
Feel what excites you and sparks a sense of curiosity. Ask questions and look for answers, clues, patterns, and coincidences. Use the subtle feelings of what "lights you up" to set intentions and guide your actions.

New Moon
Allow yourself to feel where you are judging yourself. When you are ready, forgive yourself and let the energy shift until you find a place of neutrality and self-acceptance.

MOON MAGIC

Full Moon
Reaffirm your visions and intentions until the energy of what you desire begins to feel real.
If you feel clarity, make decisions to move forward quickly.
If you feel confusion, illuminate your emotions through writing, ritual, divination, movement, etc.
Ask: What am I missing? What am I feeling?

Last Quarter
Allow yourself to feel what's working and what isn't. Let your feelings flow to a place of ease and trust in yourself, so you can discern what you want, and what you do not want.

Waning Moon
Feel relief as you realize that some thoughts and feelings are unnecessary. Intend to let those things go, and then see what you have left. Let your intentions flow to a place of release.

Dark Moon
Let darkness filter out noise and distractions. Take a step back from actions and thoughts. Allow the dark moon to reset your mind, body, and spirit with the energy of rest.

Spellcasting Basics

There are opening and closing steps that are basic accompaniments to spells in this book. These steps are optional but advisable: at least know "why" many witches perform these processes and try them out for yourself.

And keep in mind, this is a super basic "coloring book" guide to the spellcasting process. There are books and online sources that go much further in-depth.

THE SECRET OF SPELLS

The secret to powerful spells is in you. Your feeling and vibration in alignment with your true source of self—and/or a higher power—is what makes spells work.

The secret isn't in having the right ingredients and doing all the steps in a particular order. It's in your ability to focus your intent and use your feelings, mind, and soul to call in what you want—to harness the energy of yourself in harmony with the Earth, stars, moon, planets, or whatever other spiritual forces you call upon.

BREAK THE RULES

The first rule is to throw out any of the rules that don't work for you. Do things that feel right, significant, and meaningful. Adapt spells from different practices, books, and teachers. The only way to know what works is to follow your curiosity and try things out.

USING TOOLS

Your feelings and vibration are what unlocks the magic, not the tools, exact words, or sequences. You can cast amazing spells for free with no tools at all, and you can cast an elaborate spell that yields no results.

That said, tools like herbs, oils, crystals, and cauldrons can be powerful and fun to use in your spells. Just don't feel pressured or discouraged if you don't have much to start. Keep your magic straightforward and powerful. The right tools and ingredients will come.

"AS ABOVE, SO BELOW"

Tools, ingredients, and symbols are based on the magical theory of sympathetic magic and correspondence. You might hear the phrase, "As Above, So Below," which means the spiritual qualities of objects are passed down to earth. It's "sympathetic magic," or "this equals that," like how a figure of a lion represents that power but is not an actual lion.

Start by following lists, charts, and spells to get a feel for what others use and then begin to discover your own meaningful symbolism and correspondences.

PERMISSION

Spellbooks are like guidelines. They should be modified, simplified, or embellished to your liking. And don't degrade your magic by calling it "lazy." Keeping your witchcraft simple is okay. Go ahead, you have permission.

Also, it's not a competition to see who can use the most esoteric stuff in their spell. Hooray! It's about finding your personal power and style.

SPELLCASTING OUTLINE:
1. Plan and prepare.
2. Cast a circle.
3. Ground and center.
4. Invoke a deity or connection to self.
5. Raise energy.
6. Do your spellcraft (like the spells in this book).
7. Ground and center again.
8. Close your circle.
9. Clean up.
10. Act in accord (and be patient).

1. PLAN AND PREPARE: If you're doing a written spell, read it several times to get familiar with it. Decide if there's anything you'll substitute or change. If you're writing your own spell, enjoy the process and mystery of seeing the messages and theme come together.

Gather all of the items you'll be using (if any) and plan out the space and time where you'll do the spell. Spells can be impromptu, so preparations can be quick and casual if you like.

2. CAST A CIRCLE AND CALL THE QUARTERS: A magic circle is a container to collect the energy of your spell. Circles are also protective, as they form a ring or "barrier" around you. Circles can elevate your space to a higher vibration and clear out unwanted energy before you begin. Calling the Quarters is done to get the universal energies of the elements flowing. Incense is typically burned at the same time to purify the air and energy. If you can't burn things, that's ok. If you've never cast a circle, try it. It's a mystical experience like no other. Once you have a few candles lit and start to walk around it, magic does happen!

HOW TO CAST A CIRCLE: This is a basic, bare-bones way to cast a circle. It's often much more elaborate, and this explanation barely does it justice, so read up to find out more. And note that while some cast the circle first and then call the Quarters, some do it the other way around.

1. Hold out your hand, wand, or crystal, and imagine a white light and a sphere of pure energy surrounding your space, as you circle around clockwise three times. Your circle can be large or it can be tiny, just space for you and your materials.

2. Call the Four Quarters or Five Points of the Pentagram, depending on your preferences. The Quarters (also known as the Elements!) are Earth (North), Air (East), Fire (South), and Water (West). Many use the Pentagram and also call the 5th Element, Spirit or Self.

Face in each direction and say a few words to welcome the element. For example, "To the North, I call upon the power of grounding and strength. To the East, I call upon the source of knowledge. To the South, I call upon the passion and burning desire to take action. To the West, I call upon the intuition of emotion. To the Spirit and Source of Self, I call upon the guidance and light."

3. GROUND AND CENTER: Grounding and centering prepare you to use the energy from the Earth, elements, and universe. Most witches agree that if you skip these steps, you'll be drawing off of your own energy, which can be exhausting and ineffective. It's wise to ground and center both before and after a spell. It's like the difference between being "plugged into" the magical energy of the Earth and universe versus "draining your batteries."

HOW TO GROUND AND CENTER:
To ground, imagine the energy coming up from the core of the Earth and into your feet, as you breathe deeply. You can visualize deep roots from your feet all the way into the center of the Earth, with these roots drawing the Earth's energy in and out of you. The point is to allow these great channels of energy to flow through you and into your spell. You can also imagine any of your negative energy, thoughts, or stress leaving.

To center, once you've got a good flow of energy from the ground, imagine the energy shining through and out the top of your head as a pure form of your highest creative self and then back in as the light of guidance. Suspend yourself here between the Earth and the sky, supported with the energy flowing freely through you, upheld, balanced, cleansed, and "in flow" with the energy of the universe. This process takes just a couple of minutes.

4. INVOKE A DEITY OR CREATIVE SOURCE: If you'd like to invoke a deity or your highest self to help raise energy and your vibration, call upon them. Invoking deities is way deeper than this book, so research it more if it calls to you!

5. RAISE ENERGY: The point of raising energy is to channel the universal (magical!) forces you tapped into through the previous steps to use in your spell. And raising energy is fun. You can sing, dance, chant, meditate, or do breath work. You want to do something that feels natural, so you can really get into it, lose yourself, and raise your state of consciousness.

A good way to start is to chant "Ong," allowing the roof of your mouth to vibrate ever so slightly. This vibration changes up the energy in your mind, body, and breath and is a simple yet powerful technique.

Another tip is to raise energy to the point of the "peak" where you feel it at its highest. Don't go too far where you start to tucker out or lose enthusiasm!

6. DO YOUR SPELL: Your spell can be as simple as saying an intention and focusing on achieving the outcome of what you want, or it can be more elaborate. Whichever way you prefer, do what feels right to you.

TIPS ON VISUALIZATION AND INTENTION:
Most spellwork involves a bit of imagination and intention, and here are some subtleties you can explore.

The Power of You The most important tool in magic is you. You've got it—both power right now and vast untapped power that you can explore. To cast a successful spell, you've got to focus your mind and genuinely feel the emotions and feelings of the things you want to manifest.

If you haven't started meditating in some form yet, start now! It's not too late, and it's easier than you think.

Visualize the Outcome

Visualization doesn't have to be visual. In fact, *feeling* the outcome of what you want may be more effective than seeing it (try both). And try to feel or see the *completion* of your desire without worrying about the process or *how* you'll get there.

If you don't know how you're going to achieve your goal (yet!), it can feel overwhelming when you try to visualize how you're going to pull it off. Instead, feel the sense of calm, completion, and control that you'll feel *after* you achieve it.

Phrase it Positively

Another tip is to phrase your intentions and desires positively. You're putting energy into this, so make sure the intention is going to be good for you. Instead of saying what you don't want, "to get out of my bad job that I hate," phrase it positively, "I want to do something that's fulfilling with my career."

Then you'll be able to feel good about it as you visualize and cast your spell.

7. GROUND AND CENTER AGAIN

After your spell, it's important to ground out any excess energy. Do this again by visualizing energy flowing through you and out. You can also imagine any "extra" energy you have petering out as you release it back into the Earth.

8. CLOSE YOUR CIRCLE

If you called the Quarters or a deity, let them know the spell has ended by calling them out again, with thanks if desired.

Close your circle the opposite of how you opened it, circling around three times or more counterclockwise. Then say, "This circle is closed," or do a closing chant or song to finish your spell.

9. CLEAN UP

Don't be messy with your magic! Put away all of your spell items.

10. ACT IN ACCORD: Once you have cast your spell, you've got to take action. You can cast a spell to become a marine biologist, but if you don't study for it, it's never going to happen. So take action towards what you want to open the possibility for it to come.

Look for signs, intuition, and coincidences that point you in the direction of your desires. If you get inspired after a spell, take action! Don't be surprised if you ask for money and then come up with a new idea to make money. Follow those clues, especially if they feel exciting and good.

If your spell comes true, discard and "release" any charm bag, poppet, or item you used to hold and amplify energy. Also, give thanks (if that's in your practice) or repay the universe in some way, doing something kind or of service that you feel is a solid trade for what you received from your spell.

WHAT IF YOUR SPELL DOESN'T WORK?

It's true that not all spells will work! But sometimes the results just take longer than you'd like, so be patient.

If your spell doesn't work, you can use divination or meditation to do some digging into reasons why.

The good news is your own magic, power, frequency, and intention is still on your side. You can try again and add more energy in the direction of your desired outcome by casting another spell.

Give it some deep thought. What else is at play? Did you really take inspired action? Are you totally honest with yourself about what you want? Are there any thoughts or feelings about your spell that feel "off"? Are you grateful for what you already have? Can you "give back" or reciprocate with service or energy?

FOR MORE TIPS AND INSPIRATION:

Seek out websites, books, podcasts, and videos on spirituality. Follow your intuition and curiosity to deepen your practice and find your own style. And check out other books in the *Coloring Book of Shadows* series, like the *Book of Spells* and *Witch Life*.

SOUTHERN HEMISPHERE MAGIC

If you're in the Southern Hemisphere in a place like Australia, there are a couple of differences that you'll need to note.

The biggest difference is that since seasonal shifts are opposite on the calendar year, you'll feel the energy of Samhain around May 1 instead of October 31.

Southern Hemisphere "spinning and circle casting" will go "sun wise" according to the south—counterclockwise for invoking (drawing in), clockwise for banishing (letting go).

North and South Elements are also typically swapped in Southern Hemisphere magic—North = Fire, South = Earth.

So Mote it Be.

Your Magical Vision
AND PLANS FOR THIS YEAR:

Remember that plans almost always change. And... *Spoiler alert!* You can't control anything, but you can influence, change, and make all sorts of things better for yourself and for the world. You matter, and your magic and energy matter.

- Who do you want to be this year?
- What do you want this year to feel like?
- What do you want to take action on or work towards?
- What do you want to leave behind?
- What steps, thoughts, actions, and feelings will get you going in the direction that you desire?
- What does success feel and look like to you?
- What do you really want that you are hesitant to ask for?

Magic Lives Here...
And So it Shall Be!

1ST HALF 2026

JANUARY

S	M	T	W	Th	F	Sa
				1	2	○
4	5	6	7	8	9	◐
11	12	13	14	15	16	17
●	19	20	21	22	23	24
◐	26	27	28	29	30	31

FEBRUARY

S	M	T	W	Th	F	Sa
○	2	3	4	5	6	7
8	◐	10	11	12	13	14
15	16	●	18	19	20	21
22	23	◐	25	26	27	28

MARCH

S	M	T	W	Th	F	Sa
1	2	○	4	5	6	7
8	9	10	◐	12	13	14
15	16	17	●	19	20	21
22	23	24	◐	26	27	28
29	30	31				

APRIL

S	M	T	W	Th	F	Sa
			○	2	3	4
5	6	7	8	9	◐	11
12	13	14	15	16	●	18
19	20	21	22	◐	24	25
26	27	28	29	30		

MAY

S	M	T	W	Th	F	Sa
					○	2
3	4	5	6	7	8	◐
10	11	12	13	14	15	●
17	18	19	20	21	22	◐
24	25	26	27	28	29	30
○						

JUNE

S	M	T	W	Th	F	Sa
	1	2	3	4	5	6
7	◐	9	10	11	12	13
●	15	16	17	18	19	20
◐	22	23	24	25	26	27
28	○	30				

2ND HALF 2026

JULY

S	M	T	W	Th	F	Sa
			1	2	3	4
5	6	◐	8	9	10	11
12	13	●	15	16	17	18
19	20	◑	22	23	24	25
26	27	28	○	30	31	

AUGUST

S	M	T	W	Th	F	Sa
						1
2	3	4	◐	6	7	8
9	10	11	●	13	14	15
16	17	18	◑	20	21	22
23	24	25	26	27	○	29
30	31					

SEPTEMBER

S	M	T	W	Th	F	Sa
		1	2	3	◐	5
6	7	8	9	●	11	12
13	14	15	16	17	◑	19
20	21	22	23	24	25	○
27	28	29	30			

OCTOBER

S	M	T	W	Th	F	Sa
				1	2	◐
4	5	6	7	8	9	●
11	12	13	14	15	16	17
◑	19	20	21	22	23	24
25	○	27	28	29	30	31

NOVEMBER

S	M	T	W	Th	F	Sa
◐	2	3	4	5	6	7
8	●	10	11	12	13	14
15	16	◑	18	19	20	21
22	23	○	25	26	27	28
29	30					

DECEMBER

S	M	T	W	Th	F	Sa
		◐	2	3	4	5
6	7	●	9	10	11	12
13	14	15	16	◑	18	19
20	21	22	○	24	25	26
27	28	29	◐	31		

INTUITION • REFLECTION • VISION & INTENTION
IMPORTANT THINGS • GOALS

*Plant an herb garden or symbolic tree
to enchant and protect your home.*

THIS MONTH:

Full Moon in Cancer: January 3
New Moon in Capricorn: January 18
Sun enters Aquarius: January 19

JANUARY
A MAGICAL HOME

"Home" can be a sanctuary for magic. Create space to be and experience your true self. Discover how "home" can amplify your magic.

Rosemary is a classic for energetic protection & clearing.

Burn benzoin resin for luck, focus, & magical success.

Place a crystal grid in your attic to ward your house.

Draw sigils under your doormat.

What energy do you want in your home?

Write a prayer to your home. Recite it daily upon rising or before going to bed.

BROOMS — Hang a broom for energetic protection.

WREATHS — A wreath or pentacle forms an unbroken circle of protection.

LORE — Blow cinnamon into your doorway on the new moon.

BELLS — clear energy & bring you to the present.

SPELL JARS — Keep protective "witch bottles" out in the open or hidden away.

SALT — Sprinkle salt on doors & windows to protect your home's energy.

Bless This Witchy House!
Enchanting The Energy of Your Home

Simple charms will do a lot to create a magical environment. Start small and see how charms influence your day-to-day life. Soon enough, your home will become a "living" part of your magic.

First, notice what senses feel most magical to you. Do you respond to scents? Visuals? Sound? These preferences are clues on how to start.

Here are some time-tested ways to enchant your home, but notice which ones light you up or give you a spark of excitement. Start there, and always feel free to expand or use your own ideas.

DOORS & THRESHOLDS: Doors are gateways of energy. Hang a pentacle charm or wreath made of protective herbs like rosemary or evergreens. Witch's bells are a classic. String bells on a ribbon, then hang them around the handle or on the top of the door. When the door moves, the bells will chime, breaking up stagnant energy and bringing you back to the present moment. For hidden door magic, draw symbols and sigils under your doormat, or rub essential oils on your door frame.

"GRIDDING" & WARDING: Place strategic crystals in corners or near doors and windows. To keep your crystals out of sight, place them in the attic or cellar, hidden in cupboards, or buried in the yard or in houseplants. As you come across your hidden spells in daily life, you'll reinvigorate their magic and the magic within yourself.

BROOM ESSENTIALS: Hang a broom over your door or hearth for a gorgeous way to enchant your home with classic witch's protection. Or discreetly rub your kitchen broom with essential oils. The scent will remind you of magic.

Altars are covered next in February's spell!

JANUARY 2026

	SUNDAY	MONDAY	TUESDAY
	28	29	30
	4	5	6
	11	12	13
	18 New Moon ● ♑	19 ☉ Sun in Aquarius ♒	20
	25 First Quarter ◐	26	27

Intentions
Explore Your Home's Energy

Hang a blackthorn charm over your doorway to ward off unwanted influences.

Wednesday	Thursday	Friday	Saturday
31	1	2	3 Full Moon ○ ♋
7	8	9	10 Last Quarter ◐
14	15	16	17
21	22	23	24
28	29	30	31

DECEMBER 2025 / JANUARY 2026

MONDAY, DECEMBER 29, 2025
Moon enters Taurus ♉ 6:58 AM EST

TUESDAY, DECEMBER 30, 2025

WEDNESDAY, DECEMBER 31, 2025
▶ Moon void-of-course begins 7:24 AM EST
Moon enters Gemini ♊ 8:13 AM EST

THURSDAY, JANUARY 1

FRIDAY, JANUARY 2
▶ Moon void-of-course begins 7:23 AM EST
Moon enters Cancer ♋ 8:09 AM EST

SATURDAY, JANUARY 3
Full Moon ○ ♋ 5:03 AM EST

SUNDAY, JANUARY 4
▶ Moon void-of-course begins 8:00 AM EST
Moon enters Leo ♌ 8:43 AM EST

Broom Lore
Stand your broom with bristles facing "down" to welcome people and energy to your home. Sand the bristles facing "up" for energetic protection and to get guests to leave.

JANUARY 2026

MONDAY, JANUARY 5

TUESDAY, JANUARY 6
▸Moon void-of-course begins 8:04 AM EST
Moon enters Virgo ♍ 11:57 AM EST

WEDNESDAY, JANUARY 7

THURSDAY, JANUARY 8
▸Moon void-of-course begins 6:23 AM EST
Moon enters Libra ♎ 7:06 PM EST

FRIDAY, JANUARY 9

SATURDAY, JANUARY 10
Last Quarter ☽ 10:49 AM EST
▸Moon void-of-course begins 12:55 PM EST

SUNDAY, JANUARY 11
Moon enters Scorpio ♏ 5:56 AM EST

KEYS

Anoint your key with essential oil or a charm to remind you of magic.

JANUARY 2026

MONDAY, JANUARY 12

TUESDAY, JANUARY 13
▸Moon void-of-course begins 5:59 PM EST
Moon enters Sagittarius ♐ 6:34 PM EST

WEDNESDAY, JANUARY 14

THURSDAY, JANUARY 15

FRIDAY, JANUARY 16
▸Moon void-of-course begins 6:19 AM EST
Moon enters Capricorn ♑ 6:47 AM EST

SATURDAY, JANUARY 17

SUNDAY, JANUARY 18
New Moon ● ♑ 2:52 PM EST
▸Moon void-of-course begins 4:57 PM EST
Moon enters Aquarius ♒ 5:18 PM EST

*Place black tourmaline near doorways
or windows for energetic protection.*

JANUARY 2026

MONDAY, JANUARY 19
☉ Sun enters Aquarius ♒ 8:44 PM EST

TUESDAY, JANUARY 20
► Moon void-of-course begins 9:17 PM EST

WEDNESDAY, JANUARY 21
Moon enters Pisces ♓ 1:50 AM EST

THURSDAY, JANUARY 22

FRIDAY, JANUARY 23
► Moon void-of-course begins 8:18 AM EST
Moon enters Aries ♈ 8:26 AM EST

SATURDAY, JANUARY 24
► Moon void-of-course begins 4:36 PM EST

SUNDAY, JANUARY 25
First Quarter ◐ 11:48 PM EST
Moon enters Taurus ♉ 1:06 PM EST

PLANTS

"Snake plants" and cactus are classics for protection.

JANUARY/FEBRUARY 2026

MONDAY, JANUARY 26

TUESDAY, JANUARY 27
▸Moon void-of-course begins 12:58 PM EST
Moon enters Gemini ♊ 3:55 PM EST

WEDNESDAY, JANUARY 28

THURSDAY, JANUARY 29
▸Moon void-of-course begins 2:57 PM EST
Moon enters Cancer ♋ 5:32 PM EST

FRIDAY, JANUARY 30

SATURDAY, JANUARY 31
▸Moon void-of-course begins 4:52 PM EST
Moon enters Leo ♌ 7:09 PM EST

SUNDAY, FEBRUARY 1
*IMBOLC (Fixed Festival Date)
Full Moon ○ ♌ 5:10 PM EDT

IMBOLC
Feel the magic of a fresh start. Take a gentle purification bath with milk & violets.

Set your Imbolc altar with white, silver, or green candles, and incense such as lavender, lilac, or benzoin.

INTUITION • REFLECTION • VISION & INTENTION
IMPORTANT THINGS • GOALS

What is one small thing you can do to make your home a magical sanctuary?

THIS MONTH:

Imbolc: February 1-3
Full Moon in Leo: February 1
Uranus Retrograde Ends: February 3
New Moon in Aquarius: February 17
Annular Solar Eclipse: February 17
Sun enters Pisces: February 18
Mercury Retrograde: Feb 26-March 20

What kind of altar feels right to you?

Create a small daily ritual at your altar, like refreshing water or lighting incense.

Creating Sacred Space
Connecting to Spirit in Everyday Life

Center your magical practice with an altar, a place to bring the spiritual into the material world—As Above, So Below. Altars speak to your subconscious in a way that's deeper than words or rational thought. An altar can help you discover and revive magic within yourself and will set the stage to inspire ritual in daily life.

A "traditional" altar uses representations of the "masculine" god and "feminine" goddess.

Traditional altars also have representations of the four elements, a bowl of water, candles for fire, salt or a small plant for earth, and incense or aromatic flowers for the element of air.

But not all altars follow this format. Some venerate just one deity, and some focus on the witch's personal power or seasonal energy using their own unique symbols and correspondences.

While it's fine to look outward for inspiration, listen to the language of your soul and choose items and symbols that are meaningful to you.

Curate your altar as a ritual in itself, then consecrate it by setting your intention to make it a sacred space—light candles, burn incense, or spritz moonwater to symbolize this dedication.

Make your altar a place of reflection in daily life. Create a small daily habit or ritual at your altar that inspires a sense of spiritual connection. Try lighting incense, refilling an offering bowl with fresh herbs or water, lighting a candle and meditating, chanting, praying, doing divination like tarot, or journaling.

If you conceal your altar in a small box or in a private space, don't forget about it! Bring it out daily or as often as you can to revive its magic.

FEBRUARY 2026

Place animal art or symbolism on your altar that speaks to the language of your soul.

	SUNDAY	MONDAY	TUESDAY
	★ Imbolc (Fixed Date) **1** Full Moon ○ ♌	**2**	★ Imbolc 3:03 PM EST (Astronomical Date) **3**
	8	**9** Last Quarter ◐	**10**
	15	**16**	☉ Annular Solar Eclipse **17** New Moon ● ♒
	22	**23**	**24** First Quarter ◐
	1	**2**	**3** Full Moon ○ ♍

Intentions
Experience magic daily.

Wednesday	Thursday	Friday	Saturday
4	5	6	7
11 ☉ Sun enters Pisces ♓	12	13	14
18	19	20	21
25	26	27	28
4	5	6	7

FEBRUARY 2026

MONDAY, FEBRUARY 2
▻Moon void-of-course begins 5:54 PM EST
Moon enters Virgo ♍ 10:21 PM EST

TUESDAY, FEBRUARY 3
★ IMBOLC (Astronomical Date) 3:03 PM EST
♅℞ Uranus Retrograde Ends

WEDNESDAY, FEBRUARY 4

THURSDAY, FEBRUARY 5
▻Moon void-of-course begins 2:49 AM EST
Moon enters Libra ♎ 4:33 AM EST

FRIDAY, FEBRUARY 6

SATURDAY, FEBRUARY 7
▻Moon void-of-course begins 7:00 AM EST
Moon enters Scorpio ♏ 2:13 PM EST

SUNDAY, FEBRUARY 8

HIDDEN MAGIC
If you're in the "broom closet," make an altar in a witchy box that you can tuck away until you're alone. Or, can you get creative and hide your altar "in plain sight?"

FEBRUARY 2026

MONDAY, FEBRUARY 9
Last Quarter ☽ 7:43 AM EST

TUESDAY, FEBRUARY 10
▸Moon void-of-course begins 2:01 AM EST
Moon enters Sagittarius ♐ 2:22 AM EST

WEDNESDAY, FEBRUARY 11

THURSDAY, FEBRUARY 12
▸Moon void-of-course begins 2:29 PM EST
Moon enters Capricorn ♑ 2:45 PM EST

FRIDAY, FEBRUARY 13

SATURDAY, FEBRUARY 14
▸Moon void-of-course begins 8:32 PM EST

SUNDAY, FEBRUARY 15
Moon enters Aquarius ♒ 1:17 AM EST

Make a "vertical altar" by hanging frames on the wall. Try ancestor photos, representations of deities, or symbols of manifestations.

FEBRUARY 2026

MONDAY, FEBRUARY 16

TUESDAY, FEBRUARY 17
New Moon ● ≈ 7:01 AM EST
▸ Moon void-of-course begins 7:01 AM EST
☉ Annular Solar Eclipse 7:11 AM EST
Moon enters Pisces ♓ 9:09 AM EST

WEDNESDAY, FEBRUARY 18

THURSDAY, FEBRUARY 19
▸ Moon void-of-course begins 10:23 AM EST
Moon enters Aries ♈ 2:38 PM EST

FRIDAY, FEBRUARY 20

SATURDAY, FEBRUARY 21
▸ Moon void-of-course begins 6:12 AM EST
Moon enters Taurus ♉ 6:31 PM EST

SUNDAY, FEBRUARY 22

INTUITION
Set up a tarot station in a cozy corner or on your altar. Include things like cards, a special notebook, and anointing oil or incense.

FEBRUARY/MARCH 2026

MONDAY, FEBRUARY 23
▸ Moon void-of-course begins 5:29 PM EST
Moon enters Gemini ♊ 9:28 PM EST

TUESDAY, FEBRUARY 24
First Quarter ◐ ♊ 7:27 AM EST

WEDNESDAY, FEBRUARY 25
▸ Moon void-of-course begins 6:00 PM EST

THURSDAY, FEBRUARY 26
Moon enters Cancer ♋ 12:11 AM EST
☿℞ Mercury Retrograde Begins (ends March 20)

FRIDAY, FEBRUARY 27
▸ Moon void-of-course begins 11:21 PM EST

SATURDAY, FEBRUARY 28
Moon enters Leo ♌ 3:17 AM EST

SUNDAY, MARCH 1

REVERENCE
An altar will set everything at the ready to connect with your intuition. This will create reverence and help magic to come alive in your home.

INTUITION • REFLECTION • VISION & INTENTION
IMPORTANT THINGS • GOALS

What makes magic feel alive and present in your kitchen?

THIS MONTH:
Full Moon in Virgo: March 3
Total Lunar Eclipse: March 3
Jupiter Retrograde Ends: March 10
New Moon in Pisces: March 18
Ostara (Spring Equinox): March 20
Sun enters Aries: March 20
Mercury Retrograde Ends: March 20

What energy would you like to create in your kitchen?

Bless your kitchen with the scent of herbs or a sprinkle of salt.

THE ELEMENTS
Evoke the elements as you use them in the kitchen—water, air (steam), fire, & earth (plants).

SPOON
Stir clockwise to create, and counter-clockwise to release.

FORK
Forks evoke decisions and focused action.

CAULDRON
The ultimate symbol of a witch's creation & manifestation power.

KITCHEN MAGIC
THE ENERGIES OF INTENTION & CREATION

The kitchen is a cauldron of creation, where elements are mixed and new things are created.

Witches have cast in kitchens, at hearth fires, on stoves, and over fiery cauldrons for millennia.

Make your kitchen a sacred space by setting up an altar in a revered place; on a shelf, table, in your pantry, or by hanging a ceremonial broom. Or you might like to honor the elements by hanging symbolic charms: fire over the stove, water by the sink, air near herbs or the broom, and earth by a plant, fruit bowl, or salt shaker.

Kitchen magic pairs perfectly with spring equinox intentions, as it's the season of new energy and swift growth. Try this playful kitchen spell to cook up new beginnings for yourself.

PREPARE: Before the spring equinox, simmer on what you truly desire. Then write down your wishes. Gather a cauldron or cooking pot, a candle, and a spoon.

PERFORM THE RITUAL: On the equinox (or whenever inspiration strikes), create a small altar in your kitchen. Place the pot or cauldron in the center with the candle inside.

Read your written intention aloud, light the candle, and stir slowly around it with the spoon, clockwise—infusing your wish into the aether.

Feel your intention through your third eye. Immerse yourself in the energy of already having it.

Spend a few minutes to deepen the sensation, slowly stirring as you go, then bring the feeling to the lower back of your head. If your neck gets tingly—awesome. Let the candle burn out on its own (if it's safe) and spend the rest of the day feeling as if your wish has already come true.

MARCH 2026

Leave small offerings of food, drink, or herbs for deities, spirits, or ancestors as a token of gratitude and to invite their blessings into your kitchen.

	Sunday	Monday	Tuesday
			☽ Total Lunar Eclipse
	1	2	3 Full Moon ○ ♍
	8	9	10
	15	16	17
	22	23	24
	29	30	31

Intentions
Feel that you have power!

Wednesday	Thursday	Friday	Saturday
4	5	6	7
11 Last Quarter ☽	12	13	14
		★Ostara (Spring Equinox) ☉ Sun enters Aries ♈	
18 New Moon ● ♓	19	20	21
25 First Quarter ☽	26	27	28
1 Full Moon ○ ♎	2	3	4

MARCH 2026

MONDAY, MARCH 2
▸Moon void-of-course begins 7:28 AM EST
Moon enters Virgo ♍ 7:34 AM EST

TUESDAY, MARCH 3
☽ Total Lunar Eclipse 6:33 AM
Full Moon ○ ♍ 6:37 AM EST

WEDNESDAY, MARCH 4
▸Moon void-of-course begins 9:53 AM EST
Moon enters Libra ♎ 1:56 PM EST

THURSDAY, MARCH 5
▸Moon void-of-course begins 6:23 PM EST

FRIDAY, MARCH 6
Moon enters Scorpio ♏ 11:02 PM EST

SATURDAY, MARCH 7

SUNDAY, MARCH 8

To reinvigorate your kitchen's magic, anoint your cooking or magical tools with olive oil, or bless them with a sprinkling of salt water.

MARCH 2026

MONDAY, MARCH 9
▶ Moon void-of-course begins 7:29 AM EDT
Moon enters Sagittarius ♐ 11:37 AM EDT

TUESDAY, MARCH 10
♃℞ Jupiter Retrograde Ends

WEDNESDAY, MARCH 11
Last Quarter ☽ 5:39 AM EDT
▶ Moon void-of-course begins 5:39 AM EDT

THURSDAY, MARCH 12
Moon enters Capricorn ♑ 12:07 AM EDT

FRIDAY, MARCH 13

SATURDAY, MARCH 14
▶ Moon void-of-course begins 7:33 AM EDT
Moon enters Aquarius ♒ 11:13 AM EDT

SUNDAY, MARCH 15

- Mint -
Manifestation
& Abundance

INTENTION

Stir your intentions with a spoon & herbal tea.

MARCH 2026

MONDAY, MARCH 16
▸Moon void-of-course begins 3:56 PM EDT
Moon enters Pisces ♓ 7:16 PM EDT

TUESDAY, MARCH 17

WEDNESDAY, MARCH 18
New Moon ● 9:24 PM EDT
▸Moon void-of-course begins 9:24 PM EDT

THURSDAY, MARCH 19
Moon enters Aries ♈ 12:03 AM EDT

FRIDAY, MARCH 20
▸Moon void-of-course begins 5:24 AM EDT
★ OSTARA (Spring Equinox) 10:45 AM EDT
☉ Sun enters Aries ♈ 10:45 AM EDT
☿℞ Mercury Retrograde Ends

SATURDAY, MARCH 21
Moon enters Taurus ♉ 2:35 AM EDT

SUNDAY, MARCH 22

OSTARA
*Feel the energy of exciting new possibilities.
Drink tea, burn incense, or bathe with herbs like
mugwort, rose, calendula, and jasmine.*

MARCH 2026

MONDAY, MARCH 23
▸ Moon void-of-course begins 1:40 AM EDT
Moon enters Gemini ♊ 4:19 AM EDT

TUESDAY, MARCH 24
▸ Moon void-of-course begins 6:36 PM EDT

WEDNESDAY, MARCH 25
Moon enters Cancer ♋ 6:33 AM EDT
First Quarter ☽ 3:18 PM EDT

THURSDAY, MARCH 26

FRIDAY, MARCH 27
▸ Moon void-of-course begins 7:41 AM EDT
Moon enters Leo ♌ 10:10 AM EDT

SATURDAY, MARCH 28

SUNDAY, MARCH 29
▸ Moon void-of-course begins 1:28 PM EDT
Moon enters Virgo ♍ 3:34 PM EDT

- Daisy -
Simple Pleasures
& New Beginnings

FOCUS

Use a fork to decisively direct energy towards your desire.

MARCH/APRIL 2026

MONDAY, MARCH 30

TUESDAY, MARCH 31
▸ Moon void-of-course begins 8:31 PM EDT
Moon enters Libra ♎ 10:51 PM EDT

WEDNESDAY, APRIL 1
Full Moon ○ ♎ 10:12 PM EDT

THURSDAY, APRIL 2
▸ Moon void-of-course begins 4:55 AM EDT

FRIDAY, APRIL 3
Moon enters Scorpio ♏ 8:11 AM EDT

SATURDAY, APRIL 4

SUNDAY, APRIL 5
▸ Moon void-of-course begins 5:29 PM EDT
Moon enters Sagittarius ♐ 7:32 PM EDT

SALTY + SWEET
Combining salt, spice, and sugar signifies life's rich tapestry. Try lemongrass, Thai chili, ginger, salt, and a bit of sugar, or any other salty-sweet combination.

Which herbs make food come "alive" for you? Use them frequently.

GARLIC, PEPPERS, & ONION
Combining garlic, peppers, and onion is a powerful trinity in kitchen witchcraft. Use this trio for protection, cleansing, and amplifying energy.

INTUITION • REFLECTION • VISION & INTENTION
IMPORTANT THINGS • GOALS

*Cook as if you are casting a magic spell—you are!
Put your intention & energy into the task.*

THIS MONTH:

Full Moon in Libra: April 1
New Moon in Aries: April 17
Sun enters Taurus: April 19

What ingredients make you feel magical?

Create or consume a meal as a spell for nourishment, joy, or whatever you need.

Magical Cooking
A Daily Ritual of Intention

Cooking can be a spell in motion, an act of everyday magic that nourishes both body and spirit. Instead of seeing it as just another chore, treat your time in the kitchen as a daily ritual to ground your energy and uplift your vibe. Light a candle, put on music that feels magical, and take a moment to thank the Earth, the plants, the animals, and the people that grew your food.

To infuse your meals with intention, focus on the energy of the ingredients. Sweet elements like honey, cinnamon, or vanilla are perfect for attraction, wealth, and joy. Strong flavors—salt, garlic, vinegar, chili—are naturally protective and purifying. Create something bold with garlic and peppers to banish, or bake a rosemary-and-thyme loaf charged with prosperity. Even something as humble as buttered toast can carry a spell if it's made with heart and purpose.

Drink and eat mindfully, especially with herbal teas, fruits, and homegrown ingredients. Feel the plant spirits and elemental energy within each bite. Bless your food with a whispered charm or a moment of quiet gratitude.

Try using your spoon like a wand: stir clockwise to draw things in, like abundance, clarity, love, and desires. Stir counterclockwise to release things like stress, old habits, and unwanted vibes. The same goes for grinding with a mortar and pestle or sweeping the floor: clockwise to empower, counterclockwise to dissolve.

Above all, keep it simple and fun. Kitchen magic is about presence. A pinch of salt, a swirl of intention, and a moment of connection is all it takes to enchant your food and your day.

APRIL 2026

Copper pots amplify and attract energy. Iron pots ground, protect, and channel ancient hearth magic.

	SUNDAY	MONDAY	TUESDAY
	29	30	31
	5	6	7
	12	13	14
	☉ Sun enters Taurus 19	20	21
	26	27	28

Intentions
Feed your Spirit

Wednesday	Thursday	Friday	Saturday
1 Full Moon ○ ♎	2	3	4
8	9	10 Last Quarter ◐	11
15	16	17 New Moon ● ♈	18
22	23 First Quarter ◑	24 ★ Beltane (Fixed Date)	25
29	30	1 Full Moon ○ ♏	2

APRIL 2026

MONDAY, APRIL 6

TUESDAY, APRIL 7

WEDNESDAY, APRIL 8
▸ Moon void-of-course begins 5:52 AM EDT
Moon enters Capricorn ♑ 8:05 AM EDT

THURSDAY, APRIL 9

FRIDAY, APRIL 10
Last Quarter ☽ 12:52 AM EDT
▸ Moon void-of-course begins 6:24 PM EDT
Moon enters Aquarius ♒ 7:56 PM EDT

SATURDAY, APRIL 11

SUNDAY, APRIL 12

Enliven your spirit with star anise, bay, and basil. Some of the most powerful magical herbs are culinary as well!

APRIL 2026

Etch symbols and sigils into your cookware and utensils.

MONDAY, APRIL 13
▸ Moon void-of-course begins 3:42 AM EDT
Moon enters Pisces ♓ 4:56 AM EDT

TUESDAY, APRIL 14

WEDNESDAY, APRIL 15
▸ Moon void-of-course begins 9:07 AM EDT
Moon enters Aries ♈ 10:04 AM EDT

THURSDAY, APRIL 16

FRIDAY, APRIL 17
New Moon ● ♈ 7:51 AM EDT
▸ Moon void-of-course begins 7:51 AM EDT

SATURDAY, APRIL 18

SUNDAY, APRIL 19
▸ Moon void-of-course begins 11:45 AM EDT
Moon enters Gemini ♊ 12:17 PM EDT
☉ Sun enters Taurus ♉ 9:38 PM EDT

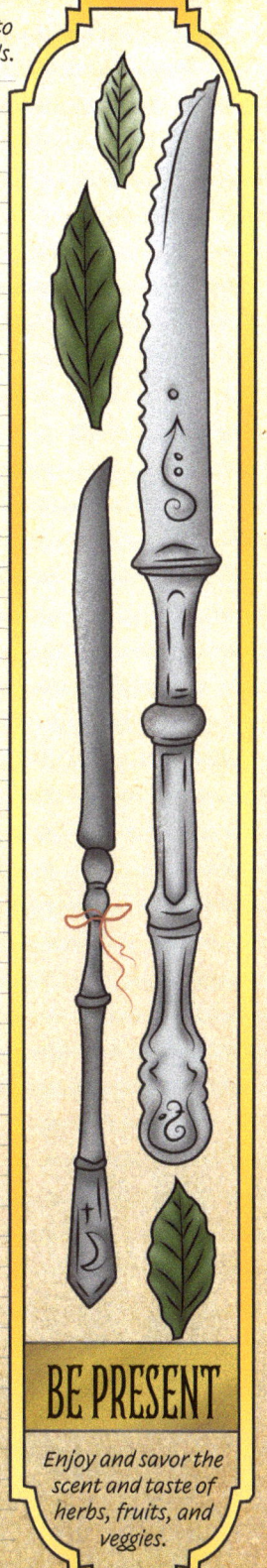

BE PRESENT
Enjoy and savor the scent and taste of herbs, fruits, and veggies.

APRIL 2026

MONDAY, APRIL 20
▸ Moon void-of-course begins 1:17 AM EDT

TUESDAY, APRIL 21
Moon enters Cancer ♋ 1:01 PM EDT

WEDNESDAY, APRIL 22

THURSDAY, APRIL 23
▸ Moon void-of-course begins 3:28 PM EDT
Moon enters Leo ♌ 3:41 PM EDT
First Quarter ☽ 10:32 PM EDT

FRIDAY, APRIL 24

SATURDAY, APRIL 25
▸ Moon void-of-course begins 9:04 PM EDT
Moon enters Virgo ♍ 9:04 PM EDT

SUNDAY, APRIL 26

BELTANE
Use food to empower your intentions. Cook with legendary edible magical flowers like alyssum, basil blossoms, borage, cosmos, and dianthus.

APRIL/MAY 2026

MONDAY, APRIL 27
▸ Moon void-of-course begins 7:12 AM EDT

TUESDAY, APRIL 28
Moon enters Libra ♎ 5:03 AM EDT

WEDNESDAY, APRIL 29

THURSDAY, APRIL 30
▸ Moon void-of-course begins 4:52 AM EDT
Moon enters Scorpio ♏ 3:02 PM EDT

FRIDAY, MAY 1
★ Beltane (Fixed Festival Date)
Full Moon ○ ♏ 1:23 PM EDT

SATURDAY, MAY 2
▸ Moon void-of-course begins 4:48 AM EDT

SUNDAY, MAY 3
Moon enters Sagittarius ♐ 2:34 AM EDT

Use natural sweets like honey, rose syrup, and dates to enchant your life with love and happiness. "Nature's Candy" is magical!

INTUITION • REFLECTION • VISION & INTENTION
IMPORTANT THINGS • GOALS

Simple plants make powerful magic! Periwinkle (Sorcerer's Violet) will attract love and protect the energy of your home.

THIS MONTH:

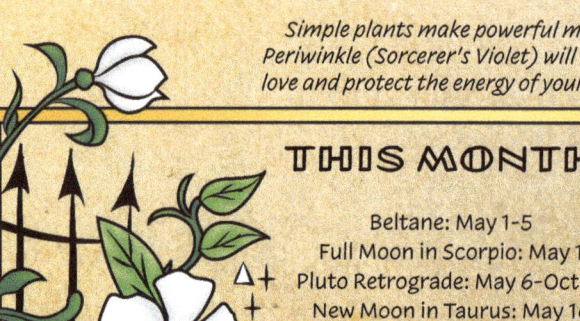

Beltane: May 1-5
Full Moon in Scorpio: May 1
Pluto Retrograde: May 6-Oct 15
New Moon in Taurus: May 16
Sun enters Gemini: May 20
Full Moon in Sagittarius: May 31

What energy do you want to cultivate?

Tend to or observe plants as a spell for growth, change, and innate magic.

PRESENCE
A garden is a sacred space to be in the present moment.

SUN + MOON
Observe how plants react to the cycles of the sun and moon.

EARTH
Digging, grounding, or smelling the earth will recharge you.

ACTION + CARE
Caring for plants encourages growth. Do the same for yourself!

WATER
Chant as you water, or place a quartz crystal in your watering can.

GARDEN CHARMS & SPELLS
MAGIC THAT HELPS YOU GROW!

A garden is a sacred space for magic. Tending to plants is a way of tending to yourself. It's an opportunity to focus on your intentions and your natural powers of magic to change and grow.

You don't need a large yard or rare herbs to experience the magic of the garden. A basil plant in the window, a mossy rock garden, or visiting nature is enough to experience Earth's magic.

EXPERIENCE THE GARDEN: Clear space by pulling weeds, sweeping paths, and refreshing the soil. If you're indoors, dust the leaves of your houseplants. Or simply visit a garden near you.

Decorate your garden space with intention—add bells, charms, crystals, statuary, or a small altar. Consecrate your garden by burning earthy incense, lighting a candle to thank the spirits of the land, or walking in procession while chanting.

GARDENING RITUALS: Tending to a garden or a couple of potted plants will give you space to meditate on the mysteries of life. Or observe someone else's garden if you don't have your own.

As you till or walk on soil, release old patterns or bits of baggage that you wish to discard. Feel unwanted energy grounding into the earth.

When you observe plants, feel into the intentions of what you desire as you connect to the energy of their growth. Witness the unlimited energy of "earth magic," the sacred power that breathes life into all things, including you.

Feel that same power as you imagine your desires, as if they've already come true. In time, you'll find that you connect to magic whenever you are amongst plants and nature, and the garden will become a living, breathing spell.

MAY 2026

Cast a circle around a garden regularly to consecrate it as a sacred space.

Sunday	Monday	Tuesday
26	27	28
3	4	5 ★Beltane 7:49 AM EDT
10	11	12
17	18	19
24	25	26
31 Full Moon ○ ♐	1	2

Intentions
Ground Yourself.

Wednesday	Thursday	Friday	Saturday
29	30	★ Beltane (Fixed Date) 1 Full Moon ○ ♏	2
6	7	8	9 Last Quarter ◐
13	14	15	16 New Moon ● ♉
20 ⊙ Sun enters Gemini ♊	21	22	23 First Quarter ◑
27	28	29	30
3	4	5	6

MAY 2026

MONDAY, MAY 4

TUESDAY, MAY 5
Moon enters Capricorn ♑ 3:06 PM EDT

WEDNESDAY, MAY 6
℞ Pluto Retrograde Begins (ends Oct. 15)

THURSDAY, MAY 7
▸ Moon void-of-course begins 10:19 AM EDT

FRIDAY, MAY 8
Moon enters Aquarius ♒ 3:28 AM EDT

SATURDAY, MAY 9
Last Quarter ☽ 5:11 PM EDT

SUNDAY, MAY 10
▸ Moon void-of-course begins 1:09 AM EDT
Moon enters Pisces ♓ 1:40 PM EDT

If you don't have a green thumb, a "rock garden" or stone labyrinth will add magic to your space.

MAY 2026

MONDAY, MAY 11

TUESDAY, MAY 12
▸ Moon void-of-course begins 6:05 AM EDT
Moon enters Aries ♈ 8:03 PM EDT

WEDNESDAY, MAY 13

THURSDAY, MAY 14
▸ Moon void-of-course begins 5:32 PM EDT
Moon enters Taurus ♉ 10:30 PM EDT

FRIDAY, MAY 15

SATURDAY, MAY 16
New Moon ● ♉ 4:01 PM EDT
▸ Moon void-of-course begins 9:02 PM EDT
Moon enters Gemini ♊ 10:22 PM EDT

SUNDAY, MAY 17
▸ Moon void-of-course begins 3:35 PM EDT

TREES

Trees represent 4 elements—earth, air, fire (sun) & water.

MAY 2026

MONDAY, MAY 18
Moon enters Cancer ♋ 9:45 PM EDT

TUESDAY, MAY 19

WEDNESDAY, MAY 20
▸ Moon void-of-course begins 9:27 AM EDT
Moon enters Leo ♌ 10:48 PM EDT

THURSDAY, MAY 21
▸ Moon void-of-course begins 6:06 PM EDT

FRIDAY, MAY 22

SATURDAY, MAY 23
First Quarter ◐ 7:11 AM EDT
Moon enters Virgo ♍ 2:57 AM EDT

SUNDAY, MAY 24
▸ Moon void-of-course begins 8:54 PM EDT

Fresh flowers or herbs will connect you to the earth's magic, even if you don't grow them yourself.

MAY 2026

MONDAY, MAY 25
Moon enters Libra ♎ 10:33 AM EDT

TUESDAY, MAY 26

WEDNESDAY, MAY 27
► Moon void-of-course begins 7:32 AM EDT
Moon enters Scorpio ♏ 8:53 PM EDT

THURSDAY, MAY 28

FRIDAY, MAY 29
► Moon void-of-course begins 8:05 PM EDT

SATURDAY, MAY 30
Moon enters Sagittarius ♐ 8:45 AM EDT

SUNDAY, MAY 31
Full Moon ○ ♐ 4:45 AM EDT

EARTH

The element of belonging & abundance.

INTUITION • REFLECTION • VISION & INTENTION
IMPORTANT THINGS • GOALS

Keep a dream journal! Dreams are a portal from the mundane to the magical world.

THIS MONTH:

New Moon in Gemini: June 14
Full Moon in Capricorn: June 29
Litha (Summer Solstice): June 21
Sun enters Cancer: June 21
Mercury Retrograde: June 29–July 23

How can you make your clothing or bedroom more magical?!

Create a space that makes sleep feel like a spell of peace.

Bedroom & Closet
Creating Sacred Spaces of Self

Your bedroom is where your energy resets and your dreams take shape. A closet holds the magic of your identity as well as your secrets and the depths of your potential. These spaces reflect both who you are and what you desire.

Simple changes can make your bedroom a sanctuary of restoration and manifestation. A cozy new blanket, fresh sheets, an herbal drawer sachet, or a crystal under your pillow is enough to shift the vibe and rekindle the room's magic.

CREATING A MAGICAL BEDROOM: Refresh your sheets and curtains with a light spritz of essential oil—try lavender for peace, eucalyptus for clarity, or rose for self-love. Clear out under the bed and move anything that feels stagnant.

A bouquet on the bedside table will recharge your space. Or place a small charm or crystal (amethyst, moonstone, or rose quartz) beneath your pillow to enhance dreams and intuition.

ENCHANT YOUR CLOSET: Tuck sachets of herbs and flowers into drawers or in the closet. Place intention-charged items like your witch's hat, robe, or special shoes near the front of the closet as remembrances of your magical power.

THE MOON, STARS, & MAGIC OF THE NIGHT: Before bed, gaze out the window and into the heavens. Whisper your dreams into the stars. Place a journal or oracle deck by your bedside for moonlit reflections and to capture your dreams.

CLOTHING RITUALS: Let your clothes reflect how you want to feel or who you wish to become. If you prefer to dress simply, an amulet, ring, scent, tattoo, or small crystal tucked into your pocket or underclothes will do the trick.

JUNE 2026

Enchant your clothing by storing them with a sprig of dried herbs or a spritz of essential oil. Try lemongrass, bergamot, grapefruit, or whatever empowers you.

	SUNDAY	MONDAY	TUESDAY
	31 Full Moon ○ ♐	1	2
	7	8 Last Quarter ◐	9
	14 New Moon ● ♊	15	16
	21 First Quarter ◑ ★Litha (Summer Solstice) ☉ Sun enters Cancer ♋	22	23
	28	29 Full Moon ○ ♑	30

Intentions
Prioritize Rest

Wednesday	Thursday	Friday	Saturday
3	4	5	6
10	11	12	13
17	18	19	20
24	25	26	27
1	2	3	4

JUNE 2026

MONDAY, JUNE 1
Moon enters Capricorn ♑ 9:20 PM EDT

TUESDAY, JUNE 2

WEDNESDAY, JUNE 3
► Moon void-of-course begins 11:05 PM EDT

THURSDAY, JUNE 4
Moon enters Aquarius ♒ 9:46 AM EDT

FRIDAY, JUNE 5
► Moon void-of-course begins 3:51 PM EDT

SATURDAY, JUNE 6
Moon enters Pisces ♓ 8:43 PM EDT

SUNDAY, JUNE 7

BAGS & POCKETS
can be secret portable altars. Carry crystals, charms, or tiny books filled with sigils, symbols, and reminders of magic.

JUNE 2026

A sprig of herbs, a flower, or a feather will enchant your hat with the element of air.

MONDAY, JUNE 8
Last Quarter ☽ 6:01 AM EDT
▸ Moon void-of-course begins 8:39 PM EDT

TUESDAY, JUNE 9
Moon enters Aries ♈ 4:34 AM EDT

WEDNESDAY, JUNE 10

THURSDAY, JUNE 11
▸ Moon void-of-course begins 4:22 AM EDT
Moon enters Taurus ♉ 8:27 AM EDT

FRIDAY, JUNE 12

SATURDAY, JUNE 13
▸ Moon void-of-course begins 3:30 AM EDT
Moon enters Gemini ♊ 9:06 AM EDT

SUNDAY, JUNE 14
▸ Moon void-of-course begins 10:54 PM EDT
New Moon ● ♊ 10:54 PM EDT

HATS

Wear a big witchy hat. The more dramatic, the better.

JUNE 2026

MONDAY, JUNE 15
Moon enters Cancer ♋ 8:14 AM EDT

TUESDAY, JUNE 16

WEDNESDAY, JUNE 17
▸ Moon void-of-course begins 3:40 AM EDT
Moon enters Leo ♌ 8:05 AM EDT

THURSDAY, JUNE 18

FRIDAY, JUNE 19
▸ Moon void-of-course begins 7:31 AM EDT
Moon enters Virgo ♍ 10:36 AM EDT

SATURDAY, JUNE 20

SUNDAY, JUNE 21
★ Litha (Summer Solstice) 4:24 AM EDT
☉ Sun enters Cancer ♋ 4:24 AM EDT
▸ Moon void-of-course begins 1:33 PM EDT
Moon enters Libra ♎ 4:55 PM EDT
First Quarter ☽ 5:56 PM EDT

LITHA

Craft an herbal sachet or potpourri of elderflowers, rose petals, or lavender. Place it in your closet or in a drawer to enchant your clothing all summer.

JUNE 2026

MONDAY, JUNE 22

TUESDAY, JUNE 23

WEDNESDAY, JUNE 24
▸ Moon void-of-course begins 12:11 AM EDT
Moon enters Scorpio ♏ 2:44 AM EDT

THURSDAY, JUNE 25

FRIDAY, JUNE 26
▸ Moon void-of-course begins 1:10 PM EDT
Moon enters Sagittarius ♐ 2:41 PM EDT

SATURDAY, JUNE 27

SUNDAY, JUNE 28
▸ Moon void-of-course begins 1:05 AM EDT

PRESENCE

Call back your energy each night before bed.

JUNE/JULY 2026

MONDAY, JUNE 29
Moon enters Capricorn ♑ 3:19 AM EDT
Full Moon ○ ♑ 7:57 PM EDT
☿℞ Mercury Retrograde Begins (ends July 23)

TUESDAY, JUNE 30

WEDNESDAY, JULY 1
▸ Moon void-of-course begins 7:51 AM EDT
Moon enters Aquarius ♒ 3:33 PM EDT

THURSDAY, JULY 2

FRIDAY, JULY 3
▸ Moon void-of-course begins 1:28 PM EDT

SATURDAY, JULY 4
Moon enters Pisces ♓ 2:30 AM EDT

SUNDAY, JULY 5

Cast a love spell on yourself. Buy yourself a lovely piece of jewelry or cozy new pair of socks.

Place a spell candle in front of a mirror to reflect & amplify your intentions.

MIRROR MAGIC

Draw a protective symbol (like a pentacle) on your mirror with rosemary oil or olive oil to seal and "lock" the mirror energetically.

INTUITION • REFLECTION • VISION & INTENTION
IMPORTANT THINGS • GOALS

Make showering & bathing a ritual. Your favorite herbal scents & the power of water will do the trick.

THIS MONTH:

Neptune Retrograde: July 7-Dec 12
New Moon in Cancer: July 14
Sun enters Leo: July 22
Mercury Retrograde Ends: July 23
Saturn Retrograde: July 26 - Dec 10
Full Moon in Aquarius: July 29

What bathing ritual refreshes your spirit?

Create a small but meaningful bathing ritual that you can do every day.

WATER
Anytime you run the water, feel gratitude for its life-giving properties.

HERBS
Explore which herbal scents refresh you.

SALT
purifies and cleanses your body & spirit.

FLOWERS
Smell a rose and raise your energetic frequency with scent.

The Ritual Bath
A Private, Sacred Space for Magic

The bath, sink, and shower offer ample opportunities for everyday magic (that smells great!). Water is the element of transformation and emotion. It is essential for life and a powerful ingredient to renew yourself spiritually.

With a few witchy little tricks and herbal enchantments, your bathroom can become a sanctuary to release, renew, and recharge.

SHOWER & BATH MAGIC: A daily shower becomes magical with a few drops of essential oil on the shower floor or a sprig of eucalyptus tied under the running water.

Salt—a witch's essential—is both magical and practical. Add a handful of Epsom salt to your bath or a small scoop to a washcloth. Mix in herbal soap or essential oils. Visualize stress and old energy washing down the drain.

SOUND RITUALS: Chant, hum, or sing to clear your energy as you bathe. Use this time to pray, ground, or feel into gratitude.

SACRED WASHING: Splash your face with rosewater to reset and soften your energy. Wash your hands or feet slowly and with purpose after hard conversations or chaotic days.

MIRROR, MIRROR: Draw sigils or intentions on a steamed mirror or with essential oil on your fingertip. Or simply gaze into your reflection and whisper something loving or empowering.

ENHANCEMENTS & ENERGETICS: Place rose quartz or amethyst near the tub to infuse your bath with crystal magic. Light a naturally scented candle, or keep a spray bottle of moonwater, witch hazel, and essential oils to refresh the space before or after you soak.

JULY 2026

Use shungite in a ritual bath for clearing, filtering, and grounding your energy.

Sunday	Monday	Tuesday
28	29 Full Moon ○ ♑	30
5	6	7 Last Quarter ◐
12	13	14 New Moon ● ♋
19	20	21 First Quarter ◑
26	27	28

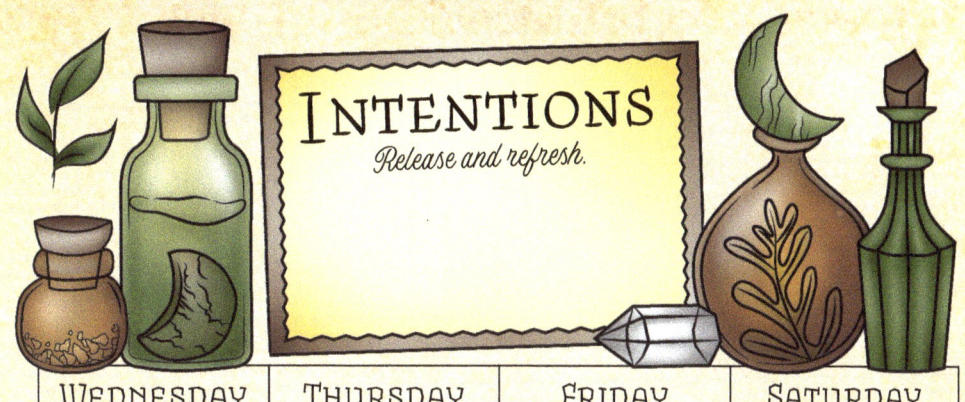

Intentions
Release and refresh.

Wednesday	Thursday	Friday	Saturday
1	2	3	4
8	9	10	11
15	16	17	18
22 ☉ Sun enters Leo ♌	23	24	25 ★ Lughnasadh (Fixed Date)
29 Full Moon ○ ♒	30	31	1

JULY 2026

MONDAY, JULY 6
▸ Moon void-of-course begins 1:21 AM EDT
Moon enters Aries ♈ 11:07 AM EDT

TUESDAY, JULY 7
Last Quarter ☽ 3:29 PM EDT
♆℞ Neptune Retrograde begins (ends Dec. 12)

WEDNESDAY, JULY 8
▸ Moon void-of-course begins 2:41 PM EDT
Moon enters Taurus ♉ 4:31 PM EDT

THURSDAY, JULY 9

FRIDAY, JULY 10
▸ Moon void-of-course begins 6:14 AM EDT
Moon enters Gemini ♊ 6:42 PM EDT

SATURDAY, JULY 11
▸ Moon void-of-course begins 6:11 PM EDT

SUNDAY, JULY 12
Moon enters Cancer ♋ 6:46 PM EDT

Add a decoction or sprig of bay leaves to your bath to relieve your spirit and relax your body.

JULY 2026

MONDAY, JULY 13

TUESDAY, JULY 14
New Moon ● ♋ 5:43 AM EDT
▸ Moon void-of-course begins 5:43 AM EDT
Moon enters Leo ♌ 6:34 PM EDT

WEDNESDAY, JULY 15
▸ Moon void-of-course begins 6:27 PM EDT

THURSDAY, JULY 16
Moon enters Virgo ♍ 8:06 PM EDT

FRIDAY, JULY 17

SATURDAY, JULY 18
▸ Moon void-of-course begins 6:13 PM EDT

SUNDAY, JULY 19
Moon enters Libra ♎ 12:56 AM EDT

WATER + FIRE
Candles are a lovely accessory to bathing, as water & fire can balance opposing energies.

JULY 2026

MONDAY, JULY 20

TUESDAY, JULY 21
First Quarter ☽ 7:06 AM EDT
► Moon void-of-course begins 7:06 AM EDT
Moon enters Scorpio ♏ 9:35 AM EDT

WEDNESDAY, JULY 22
☉ Sun enters Leo ♌ 3:12 PM EDT
► Moon void-of-course begins 5:49 PM EDT

THURSDAY, JULY 23
Moon enters Sagittarius ♐ 9:07 PM EDT
☿℞ Mercury Retrograde Ends

FRIDAY, JULY 24

SATURDAY, JULY 25
► Moon void-of-course begins 10:58 AM EDT

SUNDAY, JULY 26
Moon enters Capricorn ♑ 9:45 AM EDT
♄℞ Saturn Retrograde begins (ends Dec. 10)

LUGHNASADH
Take a bath with calendula, chamomile, and lavender to clear your energy and attract the energies of love, gratitude, and abundance.

JULY/AUGUST 2026

MONDAY, JULY 27

TUESDAY, JULY 28
► Moon void-of-course begins 2:11 AM EDT
Moon enters Aquarius ♒ 9:46 PM EDT

WEDNESDAY, JULY 29
Full Moon ○ ♒ 10:36 AM EDT

THURSDAY, JULY 30
► Moon void-of-course begins 5:27 PM EDT

FRIDAY, JULY 31
Moon enters Pisces ♓ 8:14 AM EDT

SATURDAY, AUGUST 1
★ LUGHNASADH (Fixed Festival Date)

SUNDAY, AUGUST 2
► Moon void-of-course begins 8:33 AM EDT
Moon enters Aries ♈ 4:37 PM EDT

RELEASE

Declare what you'll release as you toss flowers into a river.

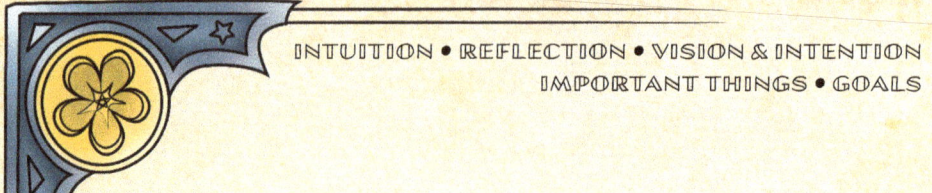

INTUITION • REFLECTION • VISION & INTENTION
IMPORTANT THINGS • GOALS

If you don't want to declutter, move 13 items to "shake up" energy of a room.

THIS MONTH:
Lughnasadh: August 1-7
New Moon in Leo: August 12
Total Solar Eclipse: August 12
Sun enters Virgo: August 22
Full Moon in Pisces: August 28
Partial Lunar Eclipse: August 28

What vibe can you create by tidying up?

Use magic and ritual to make cleaning fun.

Your Broom is Magical
Cleaning as a Ritual Practice

You don't have to keep a perfectly tidy home, but don't underestimate the power of a clean space. If the energy in your space feels stagnant or chaotic, look around. Does your home feel like a place where magic will happen? If not, clean up a little and get ready for mystical energy to arrive.

Tidying up can feel like a mundane chore, but if you spice it up with a bit of witchcraft and make tidying into a ritual... sweeping, scrubbing, and spritzing can be a fun way to practice your magic.

BROOM POWER: A tidy witch is a powerful witch! Your broom is more than a tool—it's a wand to direct energy. Keep it in a special spot, decorate it with herbs, ribbons, or charms, or consecrate it with a refreshing *pet-safe* oil or incense to help you get into the spirit of cleaning.

SWEEPING RITUALS: When sweeping floors (or vacuuming) visualize heavy, stagnant energy clearing out with each pass of the broom. Experiment with moving left-to-right or in a counterclockwise spiral from the center of the room outward. End your sweeping with one final, hearty push out an open door or window.

CLEANING SPELLS: Create a floor wash or cleaning potion with water, vinegar, and *pet-safe* essential oils like cedarwood, lavender, and rose. Mop floors or wipe down counters with this concoction, and visualize stagnant energy, worries, or unwanted vibes dissipating.

Get rid of things that you have negative associations with or no longer use. De-clutter with the intention of moving forward. Burn purifying herbs or incense like hyssop, bay, or copal to give a sense of finality and enchantment.

AUGUST 2026

SUNDAY	MONDAY	TUESDAY
26	27	28
2	3	4
9	10	11
16	17	18
23	24	25
30	31	1

Intentions
Clear the air!

Wednesday	Thursday	Friday	Saturday
29 Full Moon ○ ≈	30	31	★ Lughnasadh (Fixed Date) 1
5 Last Quarter ◐	6	★ Lughnasadh 7:43 AM 7	8
⊙ Total Solar Eclipse 12 New Moon ● ♌	13	14	15
19 First Quarter ◑	20	21	⊙ Sun enters Virgo ♍ 22
26	27	☽ Partial Lunar Eclipse 28 Full Moon ○ ♓	29
2	2	4 Last Quarter ◐	5

AUGUST 2026

MONDAY, AUGUST 3

TUESDAY, AUGUST 4
► Moon void-of-course begins 2:52 PM EDT
Moon enters Taurus ♉ 10:36 PM EDT

WEDNESDAY, AUGUST 5
Last Quarter ☽ 10:22 PM EDT

THURSDAY, AUGUST 6
► Moon void-of-course begins 7:25 PM EDT

FRIDAY, AUGUST 7
Moon enters Gemini ♊ 2:07 AM EDT
★ LUGHNASADH 7:43 AM EDT

SATURDAY, AUGUST 8

SUNDAY, AUGUST 9
► Moon void-of-course begins 1:27 AM EDT
Moon enters Cancer ♋ 3:46 AM EDT

Some essential oils have antimicrobial properties. If you have pets, mix water and a few drops of pet-safe cedarwood oil. If you don't have pets, try clove, tea tree, or lemongrass.

AUGUST 2026

MONDAY, AUGUST 10
▸ Moon void-of-course begins 3:30 AM EDT

TUESDAY, AUGUST 11
Moon enters Leo ♌ 4:38 AM EDT

WEDNESDAY, AUGUST 12
New Moon ● ♌ 1:37 PM EDT
▸ Moon void-of-course begins 1:37 PM EDT
☉ Total Solar Eclipse 1:46 PM EDT

THURSDAY, AUGUST 13
Moon enters Virgo ♍ 6:17 AM EDT
▸ Moon void-of-course begins 3:24 PM EDT

FRIDAY, AUGUST 14

SATURDAY, AUGUST 15
Moon enters Libra ♎ 10:19 AM EDT

SUNDAY, AUGUST 16

SALT SWEEP

Sprinkle salt before you sweep to diffuse stagnant energy.

AUGUST 2026

MONDAY, AUGUST 17
▸ Moon void-of-course begins 7:31 AM EDT
Moon enters Scorpio ♏ 5:46 PM EDT

TUESDAY, AUGUST 18

WEDNESDAY, AUGUST 19
First Quarter ◐ 10:47 PM EDT
▸ Moon void-of-course begins 10:47 PM EDT

THURSDAY, AUGUST 20
Moon enters Sagittarius ♐ 4:20 AM EDT

FRIDAY, AUGUST 21

SATURDAY, AUGUST 22
▸ Moon void-of-course begins 4:31 PM EDT
Moon enters Capricorn ♑ 4:59 PM EDT
☉ Sun enters Virgo ♍ 10:18 PM EDT

SUNDAY, AUGUST 23

Mix a magical floor wash with water, a little white vinegar, a sprinkle of salt, and a few drops of essential oil (such as lemon, lavender, parsley or citrus).

AUGUST 2026

MONDAY, AUGUST 24
▸ Moon void-of-course begins 2:30 AM EDT

TUESDAY, AUGUST 25
Moon enters Aquarius ♒ 5:01 AM EDT

WEDNESDAY, AUGUST 26
▸ Moon void-of-course begins 6:00 PM EDT

THURSDAY, AUGUST 27
Moon enters Pisces ♓ 3:04 PM EDT

FRIDAY, AUGUST 28
☽ Partial Lunar Eclipse 12:13 AM
Full Moon ○ ♓ 12:19 AM EDT
▸ Moon void-of-course begins 12:14 PM EDT

SATURDAY, AUGUST 29
Moon enters Aries ♈ 10:38 PM EDT

SUNDAY, AUGUST 30

SOAP MAGIC
Carve sigils & symbols into your soap or use scents and herbal concoctions for specific intentions.

AUGUST/SEPTEMBER 2026

MONDAY, AUGUST 31
► Moon void-of-course begins 3:47 PM EDT

TUESDAY, SEPTEMBER 1
Moon enters Taurus ♉ 4:02 AM EDT

WEDNESDAY, SEPTEMBER 2
► Moon void-of-course begins 6:47 AM EDT

THURSDAY, SEPTEMBER 3
Moon enters Gemini ♊ 7:48 AM EDT

FRIDAY, SEPTEMBER 4
Last Quarter ☽ 3:51 AM EDT

SATURDAY, SEPTEMBER 5
► Moon void-of-course begins 4:40 AM EDT

SUNDAY, SEPTEMBER 6

Listen to music, sing, dance, or burn herbs like bay or hyssop to clear the air and lift the mood as you clean.

Hang bundles of betony or hyssop to banish stale energy from your broom closet.

BROOM CLOSET

Black tourmaline or kyanite will absorb negative energy.

INTUITION • REFLECTION • VISION & INTENTION
IMPORTANT THINGS • GOALS

Rosemary, thyme, & bay will add power and energy to any spell or dish.

THIS MONTH:

Uranus Rx: Sept 10 – Feb 8, 2027
New Moon in Virgo: September 10
Mabon (Equinox): September 22
Sun enters Libra: September 22
Full Moon in Aries: September 26

How can you add magic to your pantry?

Connect to the energy & symbolism of herbs & pantry items as you use them.

ABUNDANCE — Anything you have on hand is something to be grateful for.

RESOURCES — You can cast powerful spells with basic items that you already have.

POTENTIAL — Things you don't know or have yet are your potential, not lack.

SYMBOLS — Most pantry items have secular-sacred or spiritual meanings.

Magic Meets Mundane
Spellcasting in the Spice Cabinet

Your pantry isn't just storage—it's a sacred space of nourishment, energy, and intention. Every herb and grain has magical potential, and when you use them, you can weave a little spell.

HERBAL MAGIC: Cinnamon brings warmth and prosperity. Rosemary purifies and strengthens memory. Bay protects. Basil invites abundance, and peppers add courage and fire. Keep a notebook or paper near your pantry to list your most-used herbs and their magical meanings.

ENCHANT YOUR PANTRY: Label jars with sigils, symbols, or words of power. Store magical ingredients alongside mundane ones. A sack of rice charged under the full moon imbues magic just as much as a jar of moonwater or a crystal.

Hang a garlic braid for protection. Or keep a matchbox and candles in the pantry to "spark" your intention each time you cook.

Place small crystals—citrine for abundance or smoky quartz for protection—on pantry shelves. Add sachets of lavender, clove, or mint to ward off stagnation and scent this sacred space.

Draw a blessing sigil on the inside of the pantry door. Leave seasonal offerings to the spirits of your home or to ancestors or deities—a coin, a slice of dried apple, water, or wine.

JAR SPELLS: Craft a witch bottle with rice, lentils, and coins, and place it in a quiet pantry corner. Rotate food with a small charm or whispered intention such as, *May this space stay full, and my needs always met.*

GRATITUDE: Give thanks every time you open the pantry door. Gratitude for what you have right now is powerful magic.

SEPTEMBER 2026

Ordinary jars of herbs like cinnamon and mint can be secret spells for wealth and abundance.

SUNDAY	MONDAY	TUESDAY
30	31	1
6	7	8
13	14	15
20	21	22 ☉ Sun enters Libra ♎ ★ Mabon (Autumnal Equinox)
27	28	29

Intentions
Stock up on magic!

Wednesday	Thursday	Friday	Saturday
2	3	4 Last Quarter ◐	5
9	10 New Moon ● ♍	11	12
16	17	18 First Quarter ◐	19
23	24	25	26 Full Moon ○ ♈
30	1	2	3 Last Quarter ◐

SEPTEMBER 2026

MONDAY, SEPTEMBER 7
▸ Moon void-of-course begins 9:40 AM EDT
Moon enters Leo ♌ 12:50 PM EDT

TUESDAY, SEPTEMBER 8

WEDNESDAY, SEPTEMBER 9
▸ Moon void-of-course begins 2:58 PM EDT
Moon enters Virgo ♍ 3:34 PM EDT

THURSDAY, SEPTEMBER 10
New Moon ● ♍ 11:27 PM EDT
♅ Uranus Retrograde Begins (ends Feb. 8, 2027)

FRIDAY, SEPTEMBER 11
▸ Moon void-of-course begins 1:52 AM EDT
Moon enters Libra ♎ 7:51 PM EDT

SATURDAY, SEPTEMBER 12

SUNDAY, SEPTEMBER 13
▸ Moon void-of-course begins 10:27 AM EDT

Make an abundance bowl or offering bowl in your pantry. Place coins, rice, dried fruit, herbs, or other small tokens of thanks.

SEPTEMBER 2026

MONDAY, SEPTEMBER 14
Moon enters Scorpio ♏ 2:43 AM EDT

TUESDAY, SEPTEMBER 15
▸ Moon void-of-course begins 11:30 PM EDT

WEDNESDAY, SEPTEMBER 16
Moon enters Sagittarius ♐ 12:41 PM EDT

THURSDAY, SEPTEMBER 17

FRIDAY, SEPTEMBER 18
First Quarter ◐ 4:44 PM EDT
▸ Moon void-of-course begins 4:44 PM EDT

SATURDAY, SEPTEMBER 19
Moon enters Capricorn ♑ 12:55 AM EDT

SUNDAY, SEPTEMBER 20

PRACTICAL MAGIC

Never forget the magic of your pantry!

SEPTEMBER 2026

MONDAY, SEPTEMBER 21
▸ Moon void-of-course begins 10:32 AM EDT
Moon enters Aquarius ♒ 1:15 PM EDT

TUESDAY, SEPTEMBER 22
☉ Sun enters Libra ♎ 8:04 PM EDT
★ MABON (Autumnal Equinox) 8:04 PM EDT

WEDNESDAY, SEPTEMBER 23
▸ Moon void-of-course begins 4:19 AM EDT
Moon enters Pisces ♓ 11:24 PM EDT

THURSDAY, SEPTEMBER 24

FRIDAY, SEPTEMBER 25

SATURDAY, SEPTEMBER 26
▸ Moon void-of-course begins 4:31 AM EDT
Moon enters Aries ♈ 6:23 AM EDT
Full Moon ○ ♈ 12:49 PM EDT

SUNDAY, SEPTEMBER 27

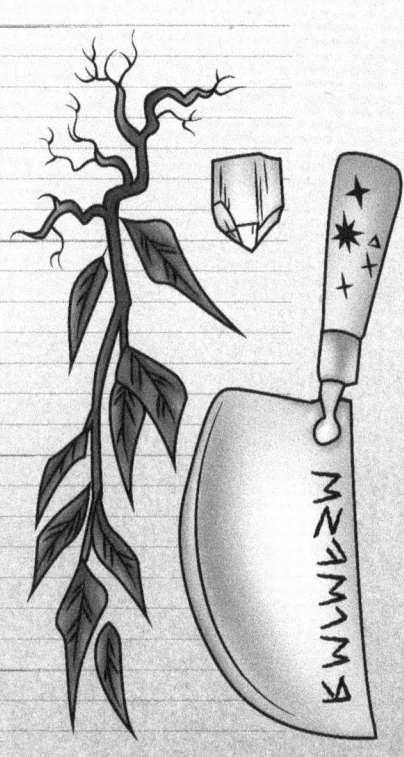

MABON

Feel the magic of release. Courageously follow your intuition towards what you desire and allow yourself to slowly let go of the rest.

SEPTEMBER/OCTOBER 2026

MONDAY, SEPTEMBER 28
▸ Moon void-of-course begins 5:51 AM EDT
Moon enters Taurus ♉ 10:40 AM EDT

TUESDAY, SEPTEMBER 29
▸ Moon void-of-course begins 7:36 PM EDT

WEDNESDAY, SEPTEMBER 30
Moon enters Gemini ♊ 1:26 PM EDT

THURSDAY, OCTOBER 1
▸ Moon void-of-course begins 10:41 PM EDT

FRIDAY, OCTOBER 2
Moon enters Cancer ♋ 3:53 PM EDT

SATURDAY, OCTOBER 3
Last Quarter ☽ 9:24 AM EDT
▸ Moon void-of-course begins 11:09 AM EDT
♀℞ Venus Retrograde Begins (ends Nov. 13)

SUNDAY, OCTOBER 4
Moon enters Leo ♌ 6:54 PM EDT

MOON HERBS

Charge your herbs under the full moon.

INTUITION • REFLECTION • VISION & INTENTION
IMPORTANT THINGS • GOALS

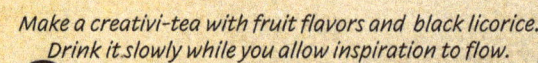

Make a creativi-tea with fruit flavors and black licorice.
Drink it slowly while you allow inspiration to flow.

THIS MONTH:

New Moon in Libra: October 10
Venus Retrograde: Oct 3-Nov 13
Pluto Retrograde Ends: Oct 15
Sun enters Scorpio: October 23
Mercury Retrograde: Oct 24-Nov 13
Full Moon in Taurus: October 26
Samhain: Oct. 31- Nov. 7

What crafts feel spiritual to you?

Simple journaling or coloring for 20 minutes will decrease stress.

MUSIC
Dancing, chanting, and singing invoke creativity.

WRITING
Words are powerful spells that can manifest desired outcomes.

ART
is not just for "artists!" Gardening & cooking are creative acts, too.

AS ABOVE: SO BELOW
Crafting is a microcosm of elemental creation. Craft with intention!

PUTTING THE CRAFT...
... IN WITCHCRAFT

Arts, crafts, and creativity are forms of spirituality and self expression. Art is the divine flowing through human hands... magic, right?!

There are many parallels between arts & crafts and magic, as they are one and the same—the directing of energy into creating something new.

That's why so much art through history is spiritual in nature. Art has that power to evoke a deep, raw sense of spirit, not only in the artist, but in those who view it.

Creativity is a powerful way to start trusting your magic. It'll help you feel the creative spirit well up inside of you and flow out into your life.

MAKE A MAGICAL SPACE TO CREATE: Your crafting space is a temple of divine expression. Whether it's a dedicated studio, a kitchen table, a box of supplies, or just a notebook, it's where spirit flows through you and becomes real.

CRAFTING WITH INTENTION: Before crafting, light candles, incense, or diffuse oils to set the mood. Or place crystals near you to spark your creativity and intuition. As you craft, channel your intention. With each stitch or stroke, vividly feel the outcome of what you desire.

A RITUAL FOR CREATIVITY: If you're facing a creative block, try a spell! Feel a circle of light around you and the bright, endless fire of creation inside you. Toss any doubts or inner critics into that flame. You don't need permission to make art; it is already in your divine nature.

Then ask the muse for inspiration with passion and sincerity, but don't force it. Take a walk, spend time in nature, and have faith that it will come. The muse always comes if you ask!

OCTOBER 2026

Ancient Celts used interlocking patterns to tie protection & magic into the hems, cuffs, and seams of their garments.

Sunday	Monday	Tuesday
27	28	29
4	5	6
11	12	13
18 First Quarter ☽	19	20
25	26 Full Moon ○ ☌	27

INTENTIONS
Channel the Muse!

Wednesday	Thursday	Friday	Saturday
30	1	2	3 Last Quarter ◐
7	8	9	10 New Moon ● ♎
14	15	16	17
21	22	23 ☉ Sun enters Scorpio	24
28	29	30	31 ★Samhain (fixed date)

OCTOBER 2026

MONDAY, OCTOBER 5

TUESDAY, OCTOBER 6
▸ Moon void-of-course begins 6:22 AM EDT
Moon enters Virgo ♍ 10:53 PM EDT

WEDNESDAY, OCTOBER 7
▸ Moon void-of-course begins 2:57 PM EDT

THURSDAY, OCTOBER 8

FRIDAY, OCTOBER 9
Moon enters Libra ♎ 4:11 AM EDT

SATURDAY, OCTOBER 10
New Moon ● ♎ 11:50 AM EDT
▸ Moon void-of-course begins 7:08 PM EDT

SUNDAY, OCTOBER 11
Moon enters Scorpio ♏ 11:21 AM EDT

*Ask citrine, fluorite, and carnelian:
What energizes me to create?!*

OCTOBER 2026

MONDAY, OCTOBER 12

TUESDAY, OCTOBER 13
▸ Moon void-of-course begins 4:46 AM EDT
Moon enters Sagittarius ♐ 9:00 PM EDT

WEDNESDAY, OCTOBER 14

THURSDAY, OCTOBER 15
▸ Moon void-of-course begins 5:56 PM EDT
℞ Pluto Retrograde ends

FRIDAY, OCTOBER 16
Moon enters Capricorn ♑ 8:57 AM EDT

SATURDAY, OCTOBER 17

SUNDAY, OCTOBER 18
First Quarter ☽ 12:13 PM EDT
▸ Moon void-of-course begins 12:13 PM EDT

MOON TOOLS

Charge your creative tools under the full moon.

OCTOBER 2026

MONDAY, OCTOBER 19
Moon enters Aquarius ♒ 9:39 PM EDT

TUESDAY, OCTOBER 20

WEDNESDAY, OCTOBER 21
▸ Moon void-of-course begins 4:43 AM EDT
Moon enters Pisces ♓ 8:35 AM EDT

THURSDAY, OCTOBER 22
▸ Moon void-of-course begins 11:31 PM EDT

FRIDAY, OCTOBER 23
Moon enters Aries ♈ 3:54 PM EDT

SATURDAY, OCTOBER 24
☿℞ Mercury Retrograde Begins (ends Nov. 13)

SUNDAY, OCTOBER 25
▸ Moon void-of-course begins 6:59 PM EDT
Moon enters Taurus ♉ 7:35 PM EDT

SAMHAIN

Feel the possibilities and magic in the darkness. Create a charm bag with iron, salt, and silver to protect your spirit as you venture into the unknown.

OCTOBER/NOVEMBER 2026

A good pair of scissors can break a spell.

MONDAY, OCTOBER 26
Full Moon ○ ♉ 12:11 AM EDT

TUESDAY, OCTOBER 27
▸ Moon void-of-course begins 10:50 AM EDT
Moon enters Gemini ♊ 9:01 PM EDT

WEDNESDAY, OCTOBER 28

THURSDAY, OCTOBER 29
▸ Moon void-of-course begins 5:43 PM EDT
Moon enters Cancer ♋ 10:06 PM EDT

FRIDAY, OCTOBER 30

SATURDAY, OCTOBER 31
★ SAMHAIN (Fixed Festival Date)
▸ Moon void-of-course begins 4:59 PM EDT
Moon enters Leo ♌ 11:18 PM EDT

SUNDAY, NOVEMBER 1
Last Quarter ☽ 3:29 PM EST

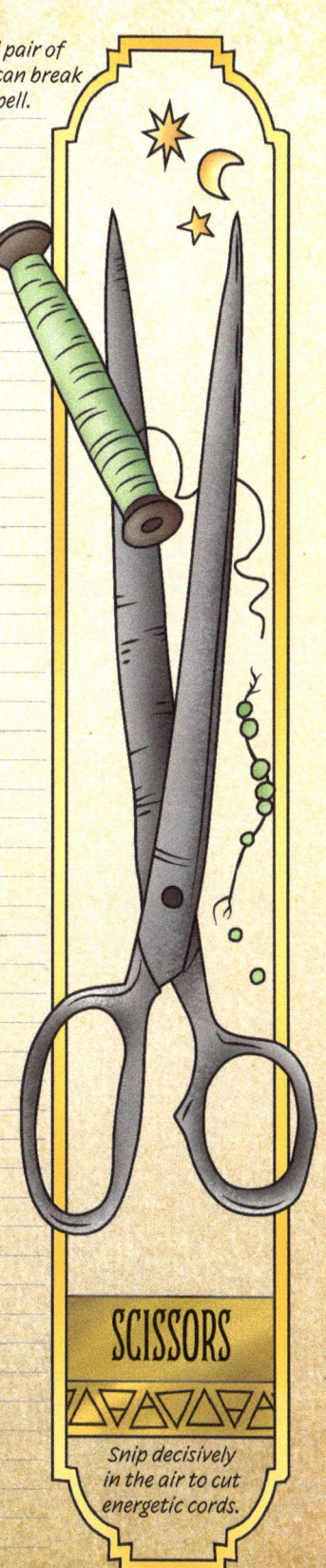

SCISSORS

Snip decisively in the air to cut energetic cords.

INTUITION • REFLECTION • VISION & INTENTION
IMPORTANT THINGS • GOALS

Create an altar for deities of knowledge like Saraswati, Thoth, and Athena.

THIS MONTH:

Samhain: October 31-November 7
New Moon in Scorpio: November 9
Mercury Retrograde Ends: November 13
Venus Retrograde Ends: November 13
Sun Enters Sagittarius: November 22
Full Moon in Gemini: November 24

What do you want to study?

Take a trip to your local library and discover one new book.

ILLUMINATION — Read by candlelight with the intention of shedding light on new insights and knowledge.

COMFORT — Make time and space to get cozy with tea, blankets, and books.

FOCUS — A conical witch's hat focuses intention.

CURIOSITY — What piques your interest? This is your intuition. Follow it!

Animals can teach us through their innate wisdom.

The Magic of Knowledge
A Ritual of Learning & Growing

The universe is always expanding... and so are you. So how can you be a "student of life and magic" and continue to grow?! Wherever you sit to read is sacred space that holds the power to transform knowledge into action, and action into dreams coming true.

A witch's study embodies these two energies: gaining knowledge and turning knowledge into real-world action. This process is magic. It is the key to moving forward into "what's next."

MAGIC FOR STUDY: Anoint your notebook, pen, and books with essential oil or the smoke of incense. Over time, this scent will prompt you to an intuitive state, opening your mind to possibilities. Sip herbal teas as you read: rosemary and lemon balm for memory, mint and licorice for clarity, or mugwort for insight.

Crystals, candles, and scents can set the mood and shift your energy, like entering a portal. You'll find more ideas on the next few pages.

MAGIC FOR REFLECTION: How do you take wisdom and put it into action? Look for patterns. What've you read that makes you want to know more? This isn't a coincidence; it's a path. Small occurrences add up to intuitive breakthroughs when you notice their patterns over time.

Write down your intuitive nudges (those whispers that won't stop!) without judging them as "silly" or coincidence. Once you see a pattern, ask your intuition these questions:

What am I missing? What do I need to know? What will help guide me forward?

Your intuition will always give you one next step. Take it! The path will unfold before you.

NOVEMBER 2026

SUNDAY	MONDAY	TUESDAY
1 Last Quarter ◐	2	3
8	9 New Moon ● ♏	10
15	16	17 First Quarter ◑
22 ☉ Sun Enters Sagittarius	23	24 Full Moon ○ ♊
29	30	1 Last Quarter ◐

Wolf energy can help you forge paths in new directions.

INTENTIONS
Learn something new.

Wednesday	Thursday	Friday	Saturday
			★ Samhain 4:53 AM EDT
4	5	6	7
11	12	13	14
18	19	20	21
25	26	27	28
2	3	4	5

NOVEMBER 2026

MONDAY, NOVEMBER 2
▸Moon void-of-course begins 7:11 PM EST

TUESDAY, NOVEMBER 3
Moon enters Virgo ♍ 3:28 AM EST

WEDNESDAY, NOVEMBER 4
▸Moon void-of-course begins 1:58 AM EST

THURSDAY, NOVEMBER 5
Moon enters Libra ♎ 9:39 AM EST

FRIDAY, NOVEMBER 6

SATURDAY, NOVEMBER 7
★SAMHAIN (Astrological Date) 4:53 AM EST
▸Moon void-of-course begins 8:19 AM EST
Moon enters Scorpio ♏ 5:40 PM EST

SUNDAY, NOVEMBER 8

Green tea and energetic herbs like rosemary, lemon, or peppermint can enliven your senses and curiosity while studying.

NOVEMBER 2026

MONDAY, NOVEMBER 9
New Moon ● ♏ 2:02 AM EST
▸Moon void-of-course begins 6:25 PM EST

TUESDAY, NOVEMBER 10
Moon enters Sagittarius ♐ 3:35 AM EST

WEDNESDAY, NOVEMBER 11

THURSDAY, NOVEMBER 12
▸Moon void-of-course begins 6:29 AM EST
Moon enters Capricorn ♑ 3:27 PM EST

FRIDAY, NOVEMBER 13
☿℞ Mercury Retrograde Ends
♀℞ Venus Retrograde Ends

SATURDAY, NOVEMBER 14
▸Moon void-of-course begins 1:56 PM EST

SUNDAY, NOVEMBER 15
Moon enters Aquarius ♒ 4:24 AM EST

FREE-WRITING

Frankincense & myrrh will connect you to spirit & divinity.

NOVEMBER 2026

MONDAY, NOVEMBER 16

TUESDAY, NOVEMBER 17
First Quarter ☽ 6:48 AM EST
▸Moon void-of-course begins 9:26 AM EST
Moon enters Pisces ♓ 4:20 PM EST

WEDNESDAY, NOVEMBER 18

THURSDAY, NOVEMBER 19
▸Moon void-of-course begins 8:46 PM EST

FRIDAY, NOVEMBER 20
Moon enters Aries ♈ 12:52 AM EST

SATURDAY, NOVEMBER 21

SUNDAY, NOVEMBER 22
☉ Sun enters Sagittarius ♐ 2:23 AM EST
▸Moon void-of-course begins 2:39 AM EST
Moon enters Taurus ♉ 5:10 AM EST

Blue crystals like topaz, azurite, and apatite can enhance clarity & enlighten your studies.

NOVEMBER 2026

MONDAY, NOVEMBER 23

TUESDAY, NOVEMBER 24
▸Moon void-of-course begins 5:08 AM EST
Moon enters Gemini ♊ 6:09 AM EST
Full Moon ○ ♊ 9:54 AM EST

WEDNESDAY, NOVEMBER 25

THURSDAY, NOVEMBER 26
▸Moon void-of-course begins 12:23 AM EST
Moon enters Cancer ♋ 5:51 AM EST

FRIDAY, NOVEMBER 27

SATURDAY, NOVEMBER 28
▸Moon void-of-course begins 12:40 AM EST
Moon enters Leo ♌ 6:21 AM EST

SUNDAY, NOVEMBER 29

ANCIENT WISDOM
Write out the "Abracadabra" triangle or count backwards from 99 to zero to enter a trance-like state of intuitive wisdom.

NOVEMBER/DECEMBER 2026

MONDAY, NOVEMBER 30
▸Moon void-of-course begins 5:11 AM EST
Moon enters Virgo ♍ 9:12 AM EST

TUESDAY, DECEMBER 1
Last Quarter ☾ 1:09 AM EST

WEDNESDAY, DECEMBER 2
▸Moon void-of-course begins 4:11 AM EST
Moon enters Libra ♎ 3:04 PM EST

THURSDAY, DECEMBER 3

FRIDAY, DECEMBER 4
▸Moon void-of-course begins 5:40 PM EST
Moon enters Scorpio ♏ 11:35 PM EST

SATURDAY, DECEMBER 5

SUNDAY, DECEMBER 6

The energy of a lively coffee shop can inspire you to write or study.

INTUITION • REFLECTION • VISION & INTENTION
IMPORTANT THINGS • GOALS

*A dining table is an altar!
Decorate it with reverence.*

THIS MONTH:

New Moon in Sagittarius: December 8
Saturn Retrograde Ends: December 10
Neptune Retrograde Ends: December 12
Jupiter Retrograde: Dec 12-April 12, 2027
Yule (Winter Solstice): December 21
Sun enters Capricorn: December 21
Full Moon in Cancer: December 23

What can you celebrate?

Set the table and prepare a special dining experience "just because."

CENTERPIECE
Add symbolic flowers, candles, and herbs to your table.

SILVER
Real silverware will enhance magical energy.

RITUAL
Toasting & praying are ancient dining rituals.

FOOD & DRINK
Research the symbolism of traditional food & drink or create something meaningful for you.

A Witch's Feast
The Rituals of Dining

Dining is a chance to slow down, give thanks, and celebrate life's abundance. And every goblet, plate, and bowl can add magic and symbolism to your spells and dining rituals.

A meal is sacred when prepared and eaten with intention. Of course, a meal can be shared with others, but there's no shame in dining alone—in fact, there is powerful, meaningful magic in solitary dining, too.

CAST YOUR SPELL AT THE TABLE: Set the table as if the goddess is joining you, especially if you are dining alone. Begin by clearing and blessing your dining space. Light a candle—not just for ambiance, but as a beacon for spirit and sacred presence. Arrange your table with care. Add flowers, fruit, or a cloth that feels special. Even one small touch turns a table into a temple.

You might like to cast a circle around your dining table (see the "circle casting" instructions in the introduction of this book) and set your table as the center of the ritual.

ENCHANTING THE MEAL: Bless your food with a simple gesture of gratitude. Say a prayer aloud or just feel into the magic of your ingredients. Raise your glass and take a sip of herbal tea or wine as a toast to the divine.

Whether feasting with friends or enjoying a meal alone, treat this time with reverence. Pour your drink like you mean it. Let your food nourish more than just your body. Adorn the moment, enjoy the taste, and let yourself feel fully present. To eat in celebration honors the magic of being alive. A witch's feast isn't just about food—it's a ritual of everyday life.

DECEMBER 2026

"Cakes and Wine" is a traditional witch's closing ceremony to ground spiritual energy after ritual.

SUNDAY	MONDAY	TUESDAY
29	30	1 Last Quarter ◐
6	7	8 New Moon ● ♐
13	14	15
20	21 ★ Yule (Winter Solstice) ☉ Sun Enters Capricorn	22
27	28	29

Intentions
Celebrate how far you've come

Wednesday	Thursday	Friday	Saturday
2	3	4	5
9	10	11	12
16	17 First Quarter ◐	18	19
23 Full Moon ○ ♋	24	25	26
30 Last Quarter ◑	31	1	2

DECEMBER 2026

MONDAY, DECEMBER 7
▸Moon void-of-course begins 4:08 AM EST
Moon enters Sagittarius ♐ 10:07 AM EST

TUESDAY, DECEMBER 8
New Moon ● ♐ 7:52 PM EST

WEDNESDAY, DECEMBER 9
▸Moon void-of-course begins 4:06 PM EST
Moon enters Capricorn ♑ 10:09 PM EST

THURSDAY, DECEMBER 10
▸Moon void-of-course begins 1:10 PM EST
♄℞ Saturn Retrograde Ends

FRIDAY, DECEMBER 11

SATURDAY, DECEMBER 12
Moon enters Aquarius ♒ 11:06 AM EST
♃℞ Jupiter Retrograde begins (ends April 12, 2027)
♆℞ Neptune Retrograde Ends

SUNDAY, DECEMBER 13

Mirrors, candles, and festive lighting will amplify the positive energy of your dining table.

DECEMBER 2026

MONDAY, DECEMBER 14
▸Moon void-of-course begins 5:39 PM EST
Moon enters Pisces ♓ 11:36 PM EST

TUESDAY, DECEMBER 15

WEDNESDAY, DECEMBER 16

THURSDAY, DECEMBER 17
First Quarter ☽ 12:43 AM EST
▸Moon void-of-course begins 12:43 AM EST
Moon enters Aries ♈ 9:35 AM EST

FRIDAY, DECEMBER 18

SATURDAY, DECEMBER 19
▸Moon void-of-course begins 11:40 AM EST
Moon enters Taurus ♉ 3:29 PM EST

SUNDAY, DECEMBER 20

CANDLES
Give candles as a gift to signify light, hope, and possibility.

DECEMBER 2026

MONDAY, DECEMBER 21
➤ Moon void-of-course begins 12:26 PM EST
★ YULE Winter Solstice 3:51 PM EST
☉ Sun enters Capricorn ♑ 3:51 PM EST
Moon enters Gemini ♊ 5:26 PM EST

TUESDAY, DECEMBER 22

WEDNESDAY, DECEMBER 23
➤ Moon void-of-course begins 12:00 PM EST
Moon enters Cancer ♋ 4:58 PM EST
Full Moon ○ ♋ 8:28 PM EST

THURSDAY, DECEMBER 24
➤ Moon void-of-course begins 7:10 PM EST

FRIDAY, DECEMBER 25
Moon enters Leo ♌ 4:12 PM EST

SATURDAY, DECEMBER 26

SUNDAY, DECEMBER 27
➤ Moon void-of-course begins 11:39 AM EST
Moon enters Virgo ♍ 5:13 PM EST

YULE
Cultivate the magic of peace and acceptance. Decorate your home with herbs and evergreens to bring light and energy to yourself in the present.

DECEMBER 2026 / JANUARY 2027

MONDAY, DECEMBER 28

TUESDAY, DECEMBER 29
▸ Moon void-of-course begins 5:17 AM EST
Moon enters Libra ♎ 9:27 PM EST

WEDNESDAY, DECEMBER 30
Last Quarter ☽ 2:00 PM EST

THURSDAY, DECEMBER 31
▸ Moon void-of-course begins 10:28 PM EST

FRIDAY, JANUARY 1, 2027
Moon enters Scorpio ♏ 5:16 AM EST

SATURDAY, JANUARY 2, 2027

SUNDAY, JANUARY 3, 2027
▸ Moon void-of-course begins 8:33 AM EST
Moon enters Sagittarius ♐ 3:57 PM EST

GRATITUDE

Feel a sense of abundance at each meal.

About the Artist

Amy Cesari

and her familiars Mr. Toad & Merlin

Amy is an author and illustrator who loves animated musicals. She also likes watercolor painting, witchcraft, and walking on the beach in a really big sun hat.

Not only does she own every Nintendo game console ever made, she's earned several fancy diplomas and enjoys continued studies in various magical practices.

CONTACT AMY AND GET YOURSELF SOME BOOKS & MAGICAL FREEBIES AT:
Amy@ColoringBookofShadows.com
ColoringBookofShadows.com

©2025 Amy Cesari, Book of Shadows LLC

LOVE THIS BOOK?!
THERE'S MORE!

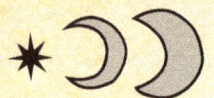 

SHOP.COLORINGBOOKOFSHADOWS.COM

Coloring Books:

   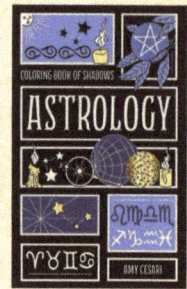

Full-Color Books:

THANK YOU!

Bollank
Art Production
& Color Assistant

Wendy Ledger
Editor
WendyLedgerAuthor.com

Fiona Horne
Editor of Magick
& Editor
FionaHorne.com

Cora
Spring Moon
Editor

Jessica Elliott
Color Assistant